Preface

A recontextualization based on a humanist approach to the subject of sociopathy. Positivists have imposed the context to leave us humanists, out of the conversation. This exclusion has left gaping holes in man's ability to come to adequate conclusions in psychopathology. Modern concepts like Psychophysiology have greatly complicated the matter, so we need to return to simple basic understandings of who man is, and what his social needs are as a social creature. This work is a follow up to Erich Fromm's book "The Sane Society", where he diagnoses the society in western civilization in 1955, using a method he called "normative humanism", in which I return to the theory and diagnostic method as far as I understand it, in a response to the question he posed in so many words 'where is this going?!' This is a report of where it was going, where it has gone, and where it came from. So by this holistic humanistic approach, I made my determinations based on empirical data, and came to the conclusion that what Fromm explained as a *social neurosis* is actually the sickness of "sociopathy", a term coined by George.E. Partridge in 1930. I explain exactly how it goes onset, and the history of the sickness and to the levels of detriment to society. Though I refer to this method of observation, I do not know if I subscribe to all its viewpoints and boundaries. I'm not sure as to the level I understand his position. But one particular place is in the spiritual realm. I also attribute the development of this research to Emile Durkheim, Max Weber, and Herbert Marcuse who kind of ties them all together. Peter L. Berger was the one who inspired me and prepared me for this unique creative form of documentation. He set me free from the orthodoxies of university, and educated me as far as the history of sociology in a book called "Sociology Reinterpreted" [Berger and Kellner]. He also brought the urgency of getting back to the "big issues" that have been stifled in research. But the number one contribution to be made is to their maker, who put a genuine concern for mankind into the hearts of these fine men of conscience. The Almighty God of all creation, who engineered man for the purpose of all creation, to extend His love to the ends of the universe, put a sensitivity in man for that very purpose, and commanded man to preserve it for eternity. These pillars of sociology were messengers sent to warn us, to lift up their voice and say 'WHOA!'. Society did not heed their warnings, so we've sowed the wind, and the whirlwind we shall reap.

Hosea 8:1-7

Hypothesis- Independence is Antisocial

Process of Sociopathy- chronicles

a. Grounded Theory- progression & operation
    i. variants
    ii. pathogens
    iii. diagnosis

b. Paradigm & Perspective
    i. functionalism
    ii. conflict
        Thesis
c. Method: Scientific
    i. Camp on Wheels
    ii. The American Nightmare
    iii. Prognosis

Hypothesis- Independence Is Antisocial

In the analogy of bread; dependence is the vital gluten that holds it all together. Once the gluten is removed, social life begins to crumble away. Independence is a cutting off of dependency on others, where social life begins to erode gradually to the point of antisocial behavior.

The rationalization of the individual mind was discovered during the emergence of individualism, and it took precedence over everything, even religion and God. I feel this is significant because of the concern of man's conscience, that we have a tendency to use this rational power of reasoning to ignore it. The simple fact that rationalization was put above God, shows a tremendous change in man's attitude toward the things that were generally in his conscience. Erich Fromm wrote about how capitalistic man says "I believe in God", yet by his actions he lacks fundamental christian values. Fromm seemed puzzled at the observation, as if it were a recently discovered phenomena, portrayed as a consequence or by-product of individuation. My experience is, when it comes to the subject of conscience, there are acts of betrayal that are part of the process of individualism. Where there was dependence, there were bonds, relationships, trust. The weak are left to fall through the cracks in the process. How can we achieve this "individual independence", without breaking those bonds? I don't think we can.

Common traits of a sociopath are glibness and superficial charm, manipulative and conning, never recognize the rights of others, self serving, grandiose sense of self, pathological lying, lack of remorse, shame, or guilt, shallow emotions, incapacity to love, need for stimulation. The real gory stuff happens when you combine the intense craving for stimulation, with psychological disturbances. The stigma is that a sociopath or psychopath is this person who lives in a shack, and eats out of trash cans, and sneaks around in the middle of the night to peer through windows, looking for innocent victims to commit some horrendous bloodthirsty crime of blood and guts. Although there may be serial killers that fit this profile that fall into the category of psychopath, it's only a micro fraction of the group that can be found on all walks of life with networks within any of the social classes, that range all the way from the dumpster diver, to the working class citizen, the salesman, public servants, librarian, politicians, lawyers, even pastors of churches and world leaders. The key component is the lack of conscience- no remorse or ability to feel guilty, or even being able to genuinely care about others.

The threshold on levels of behavior is in the complexities of influences on their particular characteristics; environmental influences, societal influences, situational influences, coupled with cognitive complexity and conditioning that determine heuristic routine, accessibility, etc. So no matter where they are in the many walks of life, they lack the ability to feel guilty, or ashamed of how they affect others, but they don't all necessarily have the same capacity for extreme behavior. In the balance of self concern, and others concern, a sociopath has only the faculty of "self concern", and an inability to have concern for others. Much of the stigma about sociopaths is backed up by the numbers of incarcerations linked to those who have been diagnosed. But -by far- most who have the condition go undiagnosed because of their cunning ability to hide extreme behavior, or their inclination for violence, sexuality, and violation of social norms are tolerable. Except for the fluctuation of apathy on the micro level, man's conscience -in general- has been slowly dying over time. But it seems in history that this is a process at different rates, in different locations depending on the level of autonomy and cultural propensities.

In a study called "THE CRIMINAL PSYCHOPATH: HISTORY, NEUROSCIENCE, TREATMENT, AND ECONOMICS " [Kent A. Kiehl* and Morris B. Hoffman], it starts out by acknowledging the reality of psychopaths in the history of man, and seems to end on this note subscribing it to genetics, but I felt in its documentation of the history, you can see its strong affinity to democratic societies. They connote the earllest writings about psychopaths back to Theophrastus, one of Aristotle's students in Athens at the birth of western democracy, and make a significant statement that *"Greek and Roman mythology is strewn with psychopaths, Medea being the most obvious."* Some of the other sources from *"King Shahyar in The Book of One Thousand and One Nights; to the psychopaths in Shakespeare, including Richard III and, perhaps most chillingly, Aaron the Moor in Titus Andronicus; to the villain Ximen Qing in the 17th century Chinese epic Jin Ping Mei, The Golden Vase."* [Kent A. Kiehl* and Morris B. Hoffman]

In all these examples of intrigue, there seems to be a common theme of rulers who go rogue. Even a religious character has gone irreligious. But that's why there's such a strong affinity to Greek and Roman democracy, and why their mythology is "strewn" with them, because it is a system that achieved for the common citizen, a complete liberation from being subject to others traditionally only enjoyed by monarchs and their nobles. It goes on to mention the occurrences in the Bible, which I have personally found also relegated them to rulers and rogues, except for certain rare instances where an entire tribe, or nation of people were psychopathic and had to be destroyed. Or even the time of Noah where everyone on the planet was a sociopath. And so this process has repeated over and over, wherever there was man being liberated and empowered to indulge the flesh and employ certain forms of brutality as necessary measures. This process is greatly compounded in a democratic society with a golden age, that once achieved, sets the process of sociopathy onset starting with absolute liberation, that eventually ends with a completely demoralized society.

Anomaly- But there is of course the anomaly of those few (percentage wise), though impaired in some way, that are unusually sensitive to their conscience, and respond to it by going against the flow in the face of opposition, and rejection, and humiliation, to not give in to the pressures in their networks to ignore their conscience. Rather, they will ignore their own personal needs in their concern for others. But society deems that there is something wrong with them, and pressures them to just think about themselves. The sensitives are now rogue opposite sociopaths, nomads who stand alone. Much of defining what social life is, and understanding the conscience, depends on us taking a look at the original blueprint. God spoke man into existence by saying "let US create man in OUR image." If we look at those words, we can observe that they come from a true collective consciousness, hence the words "US", and "OUR". And so man was created in the image of his creator, a social creature, with a collective conscience, living in a collective, doing his part for the good of the clan. Now we have to define "conscience", which doesn't seem hard because there is a common, cross-cultural experience of the natural law in man to govern his behavior. Google dictionary definition: "*an inner feeling or voice viewed as acting as a guide to the rightness or wrongness of one's behavior. "he had a guilty conscience about his desires"* Synonyms: *sense of right and wrong, sense of right, moral sense, still small voice, inner voice, voice within.*

Process of Sociopathy- chronicles of a sick society

So the actual process of sociopathy starts when the concern for others begins to give way to concern for self in an unnatural balance, resulting in us activating our rational thinking when the conscience is saying "whoa!". Structured societies take us out of our original social systems, where a healthy conscience would function normally, and place us in a chaotic environment, where individuals run helter skelter, each in his own direction gathering for himself. This greatly changes the percentages of man's concern, from a collective concern, to a primary self concern.

As modern society has increased levels of self sufficiency, so the condition of sociopathy worsens. One of the first things man noticed in his being individualized, was that suddenly everyone was his competition [Fromm 1955] *Escape From Freedom*.

Now this process has a long history, over centuries of man's social norms, becoming more and more anti-social, as he's achieving new levels of independence, he creates antisocial norms within his networks. These norms generate influences that pressure people to compromise the things in their conscience, for fear of rejection, temptation, or necessity for self preservation. New levels of sensitivities are lost in the process of adaptation. It's either you or me. In other words, it is the process of individualization that generates sociopaths. Condition accelerates on various rates of progression, from instant death of the conscience by single act, to gradual process over a lifetime, or even generations depending upon influences and characteristics. There is the process rate of the general population, and then small variations at different levels. The more recent influences that brought us to such a level of apathy within the general population, really has to do with the traditional Golden Age that follows the rush once gold is discovered within the provinces of the empire. So towards the end of the 1800s, the prosperity here in America greatly increased individual independence through abundance in resources and opportunities in industries and technology. It was at this point that the first modern serial killer Herman Webster Mudgett, better known as Dr. H. H. Holmes emerged in Chicago in 1893, where individual independence was first being achieved in this country. This was documented in a famous non-fictional novel called The Devil in the White City, written by Erik Larson about events that happened in Chicago during the Columbian World Fair that changed America. The novel depicts the magic, madness, and murder of new modern society in western civilization.

Globalization causes a worldwide crisis that leads to world war. After the first world war, there was a revolution of technology in the 20's. This period saw the large-scale development of automobiles, telephones, movies, radio, and electric appliances. Nations saw rapid economic growth, which accelerated consumer demand, and introduced significantly new changes in lifestyle and culture. There was a sort of sensationalism in the air, and there was much indulgence in many forms including a sexual revolution. Max Weber discovered the rational mind of the individual, and documented his findings in the book "Economy and Society." [1922] This greatly had an effect on the dynamics of relationships, where things seemed more shallow, and business oriented. During this time, sexual sociopathy started to emerge, as reported rapes started to bring concern among city officials. But the process wasn't as much on the general population yet. It mainly involved the big cities that had significantly less population but were attaining individual independence on a new technological level. But the smaller towns still made up most of the landscape back then. Then suddenly the process was slowed to a crawl by the stock market crash at the end of the twenties that brought things back to simple matters again. Conscience had more of a sense of normalcy by people sharing out of their poverty, and depending on each other with the basics of survival. But the nation was already infected by the disease, and the process was already in operation. Now the people were left in dire straits, with some of the tendencies during their indulgence, so rapes increased so as to have "*sexual psychopath*" laws passed to deal with the problem. That was before modern concepts of psychopathy were developed. These cases were determined to be related to mental health issues, so they were sentenced to mental wards. The disease was detected and named "sociopathy" by Psychiatrist George E. Partridge in 1930.

Variations of violent psychopaths also emerged in the big cities with mobsters and their brutal forms of exploitation and massacre. Detroit Windsor Funnel fed this form of cartel that created mainstreams of underground industries that actually helped during brutal times. Economic catastrophe caused a structural collapse that demanded the ad hoc paterfamilia form of government that originated in roman democracy. Ad hoc means 'necessary measure' that the Italian GodFathers were masters at these ancient traditions. It was in their blood. By the 40's, things were rolling again in the economy, and Rosie the Riveter joined in the race for arms, as things were back on track with plenty of work. But it was a time for hard work, overtime with low pay, and not much time for playing and indulging. By the 50's, the race for industrial innovation had brought astronomical increase to housing development, with new systems of manufacturing that created a neighborhood assembly line in the west. Millions of small town folk were heading to California to join in the new standard of living and independence. I recall seeing Franklin Roosevelt -in his response to the question about current socialist propaganda- mentioned how "Individual Independence" was his vision for America." And so the real damage came immediately after WWII as industrialization brought new levels of liberation to the general public. The post-war industrial boom included an established uniformity. Uniformity can be considered necessary during war time when there's a lack of collective identity, and the increased likelihood of civil unrest when individuation broadens spectrums and viewpoints. People becoming too indifferent are a risk during times of war, and civil war can erupt over night, *"the same man who would not think of spending one hundred dollars to relieve the need of a stranger does not hesitate to risk his life to save this same stranger when in war they both happen to be soldiers in uniform"* [Fromm, 1955, *Man in Capitalistic Society*].

But the pressure to adapt was first on the structural level, to coincide with other nations, as all were finding their way to adapt to globalization. America also took on its own form of facism on a certain level, and established uniformity in its culture; heads were shaved, creases in pants and button-up shirts with stiff collars, shoes were shiny. There was also an established pressure to meet some new monetary standard, so Mom now entered the workforce, and Swanson Dinners replaced mom's home cooking. Very high probability of children and youth experiencing emotional trauma as a consequence on a macro level due to disruption in attachment. Modernism exploded with manufacturing appliances, and materialism started to set in with car enthusiasm, having to have the latest model every year. Children were also preoccupied with materialism through hobbies that are technological, like slot cars, miniature train sets, model airplanes, etc. Meanwhile, the conscience of the parents was communicating to them that homemaking is being lost, and children aren't getting social needs. Conscience was impaired by the affectual, practical, and substantive rationality that resulted, as parents adapt to new pressures and influences, and fascinations, and time consumed in materialistic pursuits, is at the cost of interaction with family (Tim Kassar *Cost of Materialism*).

During this time, the conflict between the will of the conscience, and the pressure to adapt is noticed by social psychologist Leon Festinger, who explains it as a conflict of beliefs, and a discomfort coming from seeing evidence that confirms one of the beliefs to be true, but is reasoned away in the strife for *"internal psychological consistency to function mentally in the real world."* In the 60's, more than half of the states now had sexual psychopath laws passed, and mental ward institutions had to be developed to handle the level of incarcerated patients. Meanwhile, beatniks rebel against facism. Garb is more casual and relaxed. Hair is past the collar. Dialect is esoteric and metaphorical. Youths are totally estranged from parents by the time of the hippie movement. They dive into mechanisms of escape with drugs and psychedelia. Today on the micro level, this would be an indication to a psychotherapist of deep emotional trauma. Wounded emotions need to numb the pain, and escape reality. Gender issues are to be expected from the breakdown of roles in family structure. A message resounds from the inner most part of their being; "Love!!!". They try to escape this nightmare by leaving the system and its structure, and all the materialism behind, to return to love. But found the difficulty in being a collective while being so individuated, and with the conditions in the struggle to survive off the grid, the structure does not facilitate their ambitions to restore true family. Their message lost direction once destruction came to their lives. They compromise in the end, and return to society. Melanie Safka sings with tears about having to return (The Sun and the Moon 1975) *"I'll put on my old coat, and button my eyes, and weave my reflection in the tears that I cry".*

The hippie movement greatly increases the diseased condition of their conscience, as a broken heart often finds relief by indulgence. This leads to the sexual revolution of the 70's. Conscience receives a heavy blow as partners betray each other, and lust leads to sensual exploration. Freaks are now unrestrained in exploring drugs, and lead destructive lives that devastates families on even greater levels with drug and alcohol abuse, and children being exposed to their behavior while under these influences, including open acts of sexuality. Man reasons away guilt and shame. New levels of apathy and antisocial behavior are the result, even to the point of bloodthirsty serial killers. By the 80's, headbangers and punk rockers displayed very extreme reactions to the social dysfunction in society . Anger and rage can be seen in the faces of youth, as ruthless brutality and mayhem is implemented in slamdancing. Subjects for popular songs are dark, and morbid, with an ever-increasing thirst for deeper levels of evil. Satan is hailed, everything wholesome is despised. Agony of the soul can be seen in self mutilation of the flesh, hanging on hooks pierced through the skin, even piercing the face, the stark reality that man's conscience is dying.

One of the traits of a sociopath is shallow emotions. During this decade, intensity starts to die down as extreme behavior has become the norm. Extreme emotional reactions fade away, as society becomes more shallow, materialistic, routine, and dis-concerned with the big issues. It takes a certain level of caring that gets us to scream about the catastrophe that is happening. It takes a certain level of apathy to not even see it. Now it's "all good", but it isn't. Something is missing. Marriage is unable to survive levels of selfishness and lack of conscience. Serial killers continue to emerge with acts of torture and mutilation, keeping neighborhoods on the watch. During the 90's, war was waged against kids selling drugs. Street gangs became more militarized, with heavy artillery and regimented with codes of honor and conduct, and symbolic interaction with esoteric sign language privi to turf. Crips vs Bloods was a documentary film of kids packed and ready to kill without conscience. Disturbing cases of children shooting each other over petty offenses, like wearing certain colors and articles of clothing. The nation watched in horror as children demonstrated a lack of remorse, or guilt for such ruthless behavior saying 'that's just our life'. I recall a phenomena of self-sufficiency being achieved as early as preadolescence. The Prison Industrial Complex made prison culture part of the environment in public schools, as mass incarceration creates criminal training bootcamps, where petty drug offenders learn how to become hardened criminals overnight. Now sociopaths get an education in crime via the taxpayer. Prison owners become wealthy on their demise. In the end, the gang's attempt to prevent their way of life from becoming pop culture failed. Gender issues become confusing with millenials, as men and women are hard to discern. Laptops and smartphones become main sources of cognition. Eye contact becomes difficult for lack of interaction. Typical conversation reduced to recalling media experiences, and looking at pictures. People in general seem to be in their own little world. Mental illness becomes common, and in various forms. Man in general has become robotic, going through the motions, but lacking the heart of the matter. But now things are quieter, and man is functioning in the workforce, and has gone through the difficult transition of adaptation into individual independence, but at the tremendous cost of losing the most valuable resource there ever was, his ability to love. As his conscience is dying, man is losing his ability to love. For most, is probably already lost. Something was forgotten long ago; what was important. In our quest for liberation, man was rebelling against the voice that was there for the good. Not the good of progress, achievement, economy, but the good of man and his family, his friends, the society he lives in. As man has obtained all his liberty, he has run away from his place of origin, where his conscience lived for the vitality of his clan, and has found himself in a strange foreign land, running aimless for things fleeing him as his soul withers and his spirit slowly dies.

Analysis- this process was warned about in scriptures, and is the same process that essentially results in a completely demoralized society. During our time here on Earth in the United States of America within the last century, we have witnessed a process that has existed since the first societies. A sickness that plagues a nation, and its progression is a generational chain that goes in stages from its initial onset until its society is completely demoralized. This process has brought about notorious representations such as Sodom and Gomorrah. The cities of sin all have a story as to how they became so notorious. Lot was tormented because he saw how they were being destroyed. He saw the sickness of sociopathy. The scriptures are full of examples of societies that became sociopathic because of their practices, not because of their genes and chemicals in their brains.

a. Grounded Theory- progression and operation

Abstract- Psychophysiology in itself is a product of the complexity of the rational mind to find a means to an end. One can get lost in the vast possibilities and lose focus on the simple objective, especially when it comes to family matters and social needs. Somehow we're gonna fix all this with test tubes, and microscopes? What?? What are we suggesting, that behavior depends on chemistry? We've become geniuses in finding ways to try and make selfish ambition work. It is part of the process of rationalizing in a democratic society; that there would have to be sociologists who are critical, and then get people into a state of contemplation if we should be doing all this, and then liberalists jump in with all these highly developed rational minds, (the more ingenious, the more cunning and complex the rationality), these contributors to modern science, who just got to jumble up the whole mess with theories, who probably have a keen ability in making a practical argument against the common conscience.

To all who profess to believe in the God portrayed in the scriptures of the Bible, are -by their faith- professing the existence of a supreme intelligence, who has a mind, emotions, a strong desire, a will, that all function by the normal requirements of memory, cognitive processing, a sense of moral reasoning. All that the Almighty God accomplished in the great creation of His imagination, all came about without a brain. Mind of God who is spirit is invisible. Before we can study the brain, we first have to understand the role of the brain, created by spirit, for the purpose of spirit. The brain is very precious because it represents the hope of Man as a third dimensional creature in the fallen condition of mortality, to develop in his time, the mind of God which is eternal, through faith, hope, and perseverance in love; the supreme force of His divine heart, and to ultimately dwell with his creator living out his created purpose.

The human brain is a miraculous connection between the spiritual realm, and the third dimension, and its very purpose is for that connection. The brain can be damaged as to disable this function -disengaging from the spiritual realm. During its process, the brain goes on a journey unlikely to find that purpose, because so many of the hosts want to use the brain for other purposes. The function of the brain depends very much on the level of rational development, and the spiritual function within the soul. The brain is the physical connection of this relationship, and the actual physical illustration of something metaphysical; your soul. The soul is not assigned to any particular region of the brain. The brain is used in the development of the soul within as we grow, and then hopefully achieves its spiritual quest to find God.

The executive function is the actual person developed within making decisions based on their interests and values. The frontal lobe is where our central processing unit is, and where we develop a particular way of thinking. This is where we form concepts about ourselves, other people, God, and the world in general.

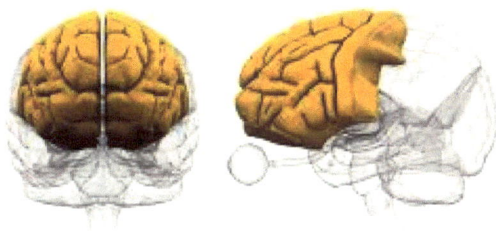

The frontal lobe is where we develop our complex cognitive structure through social networking. This is first and foremost the place where we are either developed, or underdeveloped socially. The point is to mentally be compatible with the moral force of spirit. We can detect by neuroimaging activity in certain regions, and chemicals flowing, but the actual thoughts can't be captured in a vial, or detected by thermal imaging equipment. Like seeing the leaves moving, but not capturing the essence of the wind. They are invisible and something only experienced within the soul. The thermal fluctuation and chemical activations are just responses that have to do with making the physiological connection, for tasks and interaction. So that would make the soul and spirit the governor, and not the brain. If we are led by a strong moral force of spirit, then it is spirit that is the governor and who we truly are. External forces can affect this governance of soul and spirit. Sociopathy is a process of replacing values as motivators that gradually go from the governance of spirit, to being led by flesh. That is when the brain becomes the governor. We literally become materialized. The positivist approach seems to be trying to leave out the "spiritual", or "metaphysical" part of man that can't be seen by the naked eye. This perspective declares, by modern concepts, that there is no God or spiritual realm, and that all existence is confined within the laws of physics. Positivism is a form of hyper-rationalization that comes from total estrangement of social reality. Humanistic purposes for brain imaging wouldn't abandon the natural holistic needs of healthy social development, to turn to pharmaceutical and institutional alternatives that replace wholesome upbringing and socialization. Process of sociopathy has grown into a techno version.

Reduction of neuroactivity is detected at the Amygdala by neuroimaging for all four of the correlating factors of sociopathy- Interpersonal, affect, antisocial, and lifestyle. Neuroimaging for Interpersonal negative emotional response include reductions in the Ventromedial Prefrontal Cortex, Angular Gyrus, and the Posterior Cingulate Gyrus [*2008 The neural correlates of moral decision-making in psychopathy A L Glenn, A Raine & R A Schug*]. See data

So the "*ethical rationality memorization of rules for proper conduct*" replaces simple affectual sensitivity of conscience. This will result in irregularity of neuro-activity between the ventromedial prefrontal cortex, and the amygdala. "*The right posterior VLPFC (BA 44) is active during the updating of action plans. The right middle VLPFC (BA 45) responds to decision uncertainty (presumably in right-handed individuals``[Levy, BJ; Wagner, AD (2004)]*]. But this is dictated by the executive function based on interests and values, and then habitualized into an automation when social rationality bypasses the Affect at the Amygdala. The Amygdala is a central accessing point of emotional sensory and moral charge initially intended to be primary in decision making. Rational development disrupts this function in decisions, and -by choice- avoids the emotional sensory when executing action. The amygdala is the two ball shaped sensors at the end of the stems on both sides. Our spirit has to be born in this place. This is where our conscious spirit is implemented in decision making by this sensory input. It is when the amygdala senses a void, or has an intermediate interference in communications, that this point of connection to the central medial cortex becomes redundant in decision making, and you lose moral force in action, and emotions are reduced to stimuli that become routine. It is in the sensory of spirit, that brings the things that come from spirit, which are all part of the building blocks of love.

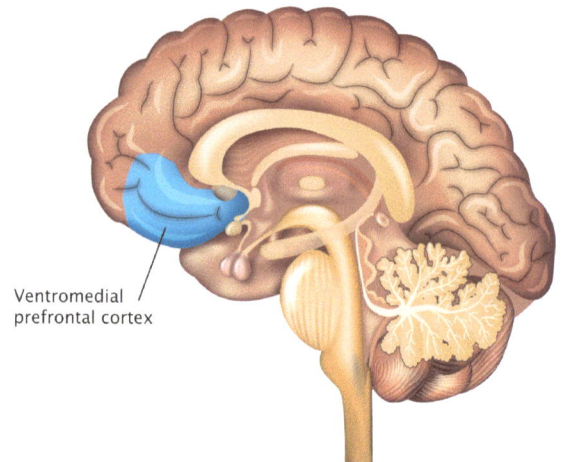

Ventromedial prefrontal cortex

So the moral development to love is actually the development of our spirit resulting in Affect. At this point where our conscience is aware, we have to choose when we are ready to go to this holy place to clear our conscience. This reluctance comes from a complacency while in a rational fantasy. We lose our awareness when we bypass the still small voice. Then we end up with rationalized rituals and materialistic gods. This is a sign of a spiritual vacuum. Physiological damage at anypoint of the VMPFC, AMG, ANG, or PCG can disrupt this relationship to access sensitivity at the amygdala in decision making. Rational fantasy can also disrupt this relationship. Brain imaging is irrelevant at that point- opportunity is in the duration of transvaluation of values. All social existence is spiritual, and so needs a spiritual approach. The more materialistic we become, the more we are discerned from spiritual, and man becomes commodified down to tissue, chemistry, and biological mechanisms.

So what is spiritual? To define the word, we will look at the most reliable source of spiritual understanding; the Holy Bible. God is the Almighty Creator Yahweh; the Spirit of Love (1 Jn 4:8). Scriptures that apply to love include concepts and various expressions of love: care, appreciation, concern, understanding, encouragement, trust, forbearance, mercy, humility, kindness, faithfulness, compassion, gentleness, forgiveness, consideration, having hope for others, having self control, sharing of resources, generosity, respect, intimacy, companionship. These are what I call "spiritual". *"The goal of this command is love, which comes from a pure heart and a good conscience"* [1 Tim 1:5]. All these traits of expression come from the communion of a healthy sober spirit, in a healthy soul whose actions are in congruence with their conscience. Psychiatrist Adolf Guggenbuhl-Craig referred to a psychopath as an *"empty soul".* This is an indication that Adolf was observing a void, an absence, lack of presence, or occupant. This absence is a metaphysical one. But we have to consider the possibility that our awareness includes a spiritual awakeness. So the phrase "nobody's home", would be an actual case of them being home, but not awake to answer the door. In observance of the brain -not as governor but as slave to the executive- the affective function begins at the amygdala, located in the medial temporal lobe in the central part of the brain.

The amygdala is the receptor and physiological sensory of conscious spirit. This brain function is for the purpose of expressing love in decision making. Expression of spirit is necessary for healthy social life in all spheres of society. This special place is where the moral force is present, or not present. Spirit is like a seed- has to be planted in this place of the soul by another spirit, generally from father and mother during nurturing. There's a receptive part of this function that receives the seed of the spirit, and hopefully at some point brought out of its dormant state through strong representations and confrontations to finally reach the ovum, to spring its radical shoot and through faith and patient endurance brings about its fruition to function as a maturing spirit. Normal stage for this is adolescence. Soul of the individual has to be in communion with his spirit for this function at the amygdala to be in sound operation. To the degree the soul is educated in this congruence, determines the level of spiritual prosperity and social health even unto godliness. This is how the connection is made from the third dimension, to the spiritual realm. The sensory of our spirit at the amygdala accesses recorded memories stored in the schema of the hippocampus. A healthy conscience of spirit will bring us back when we've drifted from our moral obligations. This drifting is when there is deliberation in a conflict of values. Values that conflict with the moral force of spirit. When realized, we can come to a contriteness, as Fromm said about our conscience that it "*brings us back to ourselves.*" The forming of our spirit is the essence of true self. If the moral force of spirit isn't watering our soul, and nourished in the ways that cause us to grow in loving others, our soul begins to wither and die.

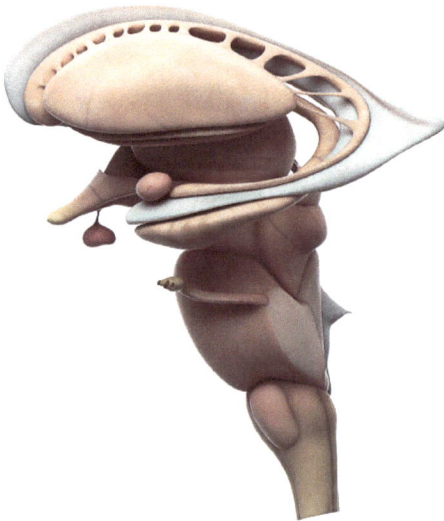

Our spirit is able to access the schema for memories stored in the hippocampus, those special moments of times with family, and friends. That is the grayish white matter that goes along and cradles the amygdala stem. This is where true love can grow, and be nourished. But this is also where we can be hurt, even fatally hurt. Spirit can die. Healing emotional wounds is a very careful technique of reprocessing the schema. This generally has to cover the basic timeline of trauma, PTSD and Complex.

Slipping away- It is part of the development of love; that one goes through periods of slipping away from what mommy and daddy have been teaching them. And because it was from the expression of true love, it is from their spirit. So the conviction of their realization of the guilt, a healthy soul not prone to rationalizing will face the reality of their guilt, and the awakened soul now becomes contrite. But it was because you were so loved, and mommy and daddy are so much a part of teaching you, and taking care of you. Sharing so many moments, they become your everything. And you develop this deep desire to please them- to be a good son or good daughter because you know this means everything to them. A healthy soul has this special place in their most shining stars- the highest of their values. That's when the moral force of conscience at the amygdala is paramount in decision making- this extends to God later.

Our rationally developed minds are prone to this slipping away, but once touched by moral conviction through confrontation, or memory triggered by the situation, spirit awakens from its slumber and is brought back to its senses, often opening a well of deep emotions. These are triggered by meaningful memories recorded of events that were spiritual; moments that were vital to the growth of the spirit, and so are metaphysical. This contrite response brings about a cleansing of the conscience of guilt, and a restoration of the communion of spirit and soul. The brain function of the amygdala is for the purpose of expressions of love, but not the source of their expressions. The source of true love and tenderness comes from spirit. The Angular gyrus is also vitally interactive with the prefrontal cortex- the seat of the "executive function", where we govern our interactions according to our motivations. Rationalities can disrupt this function at the MPF, and condition the mind to programmed automations of actions when we bypass the Affect. This bypassing results in a voxel reduction at the amygdala, and the medial prefrontal cortex. So the relationship of spirit and soul is much like the relationship between monarch and bishop. Monarch is the executive power, but should be humble enough to defer to his spiritual adviser before deliberating his plan of action.

Angular gyrus

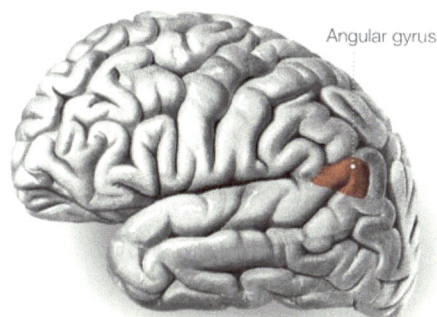

Angular gyrus

Angular gyrus is the point of the circuit that the spirit uses for interpreting outside forces, communicating to the spirit as well as executive awareness. If we are placing the wrong definitions on actions, it is a disruption by semantic breakdown. It is like lying to the spirit about what's really going on. There is a potential of screening the reality of the situations, by rationality disrupting the spiritual involvement in action by rationally taking it out of the 'moral' spectrum. The angular gyrus is part of the inferior parietal lobe. This is part of the somatic sensory system that includes the interpretation of words and their meanings in establishing semantics of language, which helps with reasoning processed in the medial prefrontal cortex. Angular gyrus also interprets symbols, mathematical problems, but most significantly in this sense, the decoding and solving of puzzles. This works in conjunction with the VMPFC, AMG, and ANG. It is the connection point where rationality disrupts this interpretation, and moral programming by placing the wrong definition on actions and words. Strong social construct of reality and cognitive complexity is essential for this part of the brain to be in sound operation. These vitally important parts of the brain for healthy decision making are all part of the complex limbic system starting at the midbrain, also known as the reptilian brain.. This system is made up of three stages of development, L1, L2, and L3.

L1 is the beginning of our brain, established in our infancy while we are in survival mode. L2 begins in our emotional development years. This is primary for establishing healthy decision making in later years. They must learn during toddler years, to be emotionally content with their given space and things. They must learn to not violate the other children, and establish emotional boundaries they need for social development that begins during the oedipus stage- 4 - 6 years of age. Also vital gender association is established during this time, which includes developing a protective loving side of the opposite sex. This demands healthy involvement of both parents who truly love each other. L3 is where our higher cognitive development is, where we have our logical reasoning, and understanding of social complexities. The survival mode L1 -evoked by fear- suddenly takes us out of our logical and reasoning functions of L3, and puts us in a fight or flight state that is unstable and impulsive. We can also revert to L2 during emotional dilemmas. This can be caused from unresolved emotional pain in need of cognitive emotional behavioral therapy.

Hypothesis on the PCC- Posterior Cingulate Cortex; *"dorsal and ventral parts of the PCC and propose that the function of these subcomponents can be explained by considering: (i) arousal state; (ii) whether attention is focused internally or externally; and (iii) the breadth of attentional focus (ABBA: Arousal, Balance and Breadth of Attention model). [Robert Leech, David J. Sharp 2013]* "The neuroimaging detects activity during certain moments that seem to suggest the PCC is a sort of pre-brain in its initial development, involving attention span which is developed beginning at infancy. Once the infant is able to see clearly, his education begins with facial and vocal interactions that gain their attention. As we interact in these ways, they are learning and increasing their attention span as they learn. Attention span has to be developed socially. It is by this investment of love that affects the internal and external focus rate.

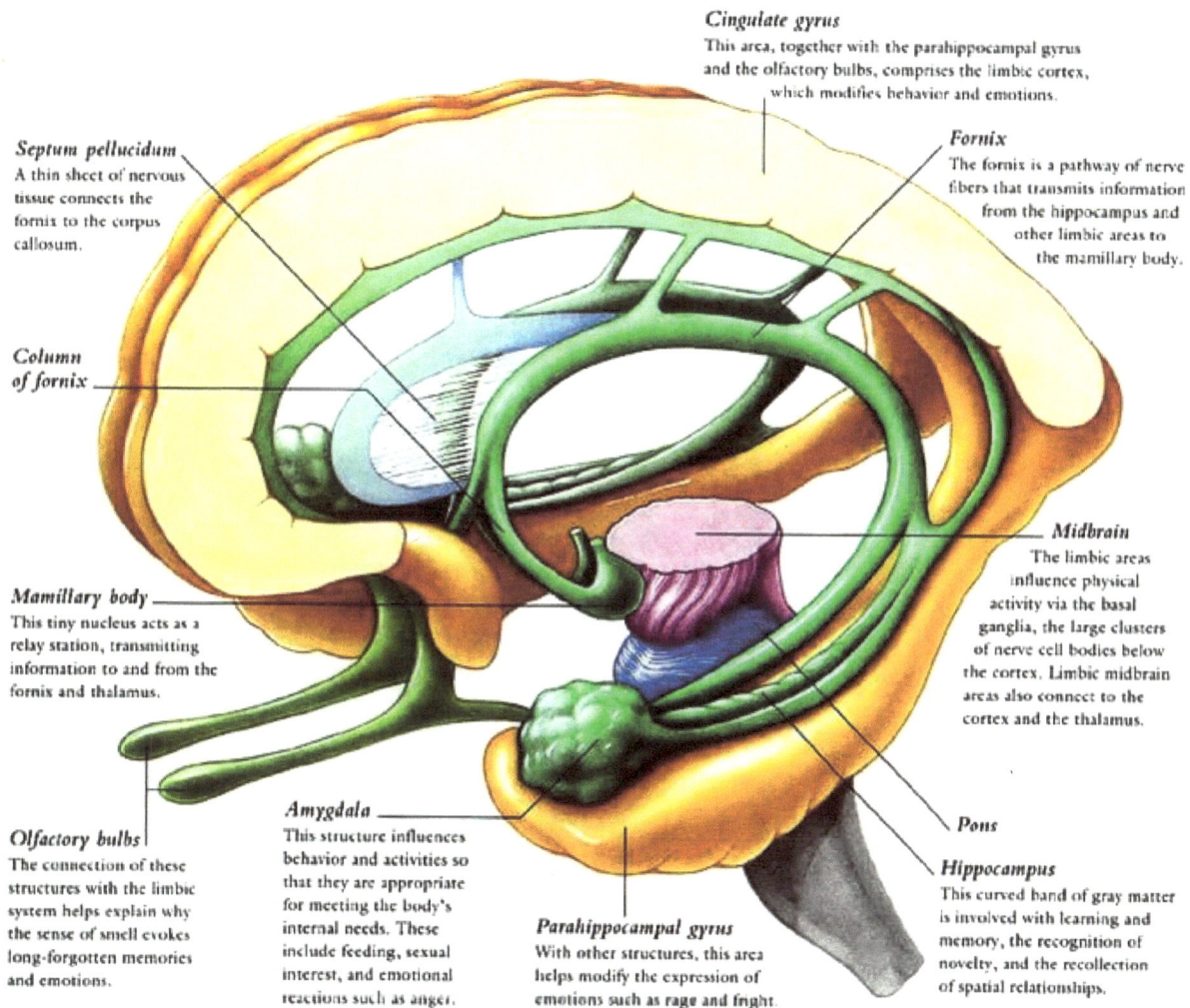

Cingulate gyrus
This area, together with the parahippocampal gyrus and the olfactory bulbs, comprises the limbic cortex, which modifies behavior and emotions.

Septum pellucidum
A thin sheet of nervous tissue connects the fornix to the corpus callosum.

Fornix
The fornix is a pathway of nerve fibers that transmits information from the hippocampus and other limbic areas to the mamillary body.

Column of fornix

Mamillary body
This tiny nucleus acts as a relay station, transmitting information to and from the fornix and thalamus.

Midbrain
The limbic areas influence physical activity via the basal ganglia, the large clusters of nerve cell bodies below the cortex. Limbic midbrain areas also connect to the cortex and the thalamus.

Olfactory bulbs
The connection of these structures with the limbic system helps explain why the sense of smell evokes long-forgotten memories and emotions.

Amygdala
This structure influences behavior and activities so that they are appropriate for meeting the body's internal needs. These include feeding, sexual interest, and emotional reactions such as anger.

Parahippocampal gyrus
With other structures, this area helps modify the expression of emotions such as rage and fright.

Pons

Hippocampus
This curved band of gray matter is involved with learning and memory, the recognition of novelty, and the recollection of spatial relationships.

The cingulate gyrus is referred to as the "behavior modifier." Another indication of its role in early development is its heightened activity when recalling autobiographical memories. This would involve accessing a private vault of memories during times of these vital investments stored in the hippocampus schema. ADD is generally a deficit of interaction at this vital point of development. Attention span is a social development that must carry on to deeper levels of investment. This even establishes their ability of planning tasks in coordination with the right posterior VLPFC (BA 44) . This is where we can either establish an interdependent deliberation that is group oriented, or a self centered deliberation from materialistic interests. This would be the point affected by value and instrumental (means-end) rationality in the liberation pathway to revert to NP-II, secondary narcissism, and onto primary interpersonal sociopath. The interactions with the right middle VLPFC (BA 45), involve groping in uncertainty, is the point where affectual rationality can desensitize conscience, by unconditioned responses to exposure. It is by the things we focus on, and these moments of uncertainty that we reason away what our conscience is trying to communicate. This is where the amygdala's participation depends on accurate communication from the angular gyrus in the interpretation of semantics and actions. We can process inaccurate conclusions during emotional dilemmas and remove subjectivity to moral obligation. This lulls our soul to sleep. *Actions have to be real in their definitions, to be real in their consequences.* Our soul can be awakened by the spirit of an awakened soul, if there's still some gap in the rational fantasy, and the transvaluation still not gone to its completion. Some level of moral value still has to remain, or spirit is absent. As this function diminishes, usually over generations, man's life becomes automated, depending on programmed routine modes of operation and interaction, daily ritual, coupled with acquired tastes and cravings. It is the healthy interaction between the spirit and executive function that brings the spice of life, with poetic spontaneity and character. Without this attribute, we might not even be human anymore. What is man? Though we share similarities, the differences are extreme. The *automaton* is a sort of doppelganger autopilot. This phenomena can happen within a single lifespan. Some have experienced seeing this transition to doppelganger and will state with universal agreement, "*it was like they became a completely different person.*" A common occurrence would be the rock-star syndrome. So the spirit of the person can die within the soul, and leave its vessel to operate in a sort of default mode. A dying spirit slowly becomes an evil spirit. Those who didn't respond to the still small voice of conscience, but continued to rationalize away their affective sensitivity, were left unaccountable and unreachable in their fantasy. There is a certain point when a spirit can be commanded to awaken from death.

Heuristic cognitive breakdown- the irregularities in heuristics come from the internalization of society, that is too vast to know all the complexities relating to typification. We're designed for small groups who are all familiar with each other, that gives us security and assurance with the ones who surround our lives. Primary self concern compounds distance between individuals. Lazy minds, self absorbed and preoccupied with various forms of stimulation, lack necessary motivation. A child cannot develop on his own a complex enough structure for normal cognitive processing. Our realities and motivations are *socially constructed*. This motivation would generally come from the enthusiasm of a child to feed off the parents' investment, as well as the other members of the clan. This vital attribute of enthusiasm is unlikely to occur when parents are absent during important moments that would communicate love and importance. Dependence of clan living demands investment in children, that communicates to them they are vitally important to all. This encouragement spurs them in moments to act with corrective emotional responses that are signs of new maturity. This is all part of developing a healthy cluster of values that have to be all in order by the time of adulthood. These values are intertwined with their adoration and love for mom and dad and family. These important parts of relationships are what satisfy the soul. It is when we miss these valuable moments and relationships, that we sense a void that we try to fill with other things that never truly satisfy. Mass consumption is the spiritual starvation of the soul in man, that creates a void with an insatiable need to stimulate. Materialistic pursuit is a dismal and mundane existence that we try to paint as important or meaningful, and make it look like family and friends. When the core of a social creature's being is removed, it changes everything about him; the way his brain functions, his metabolism, proper limbic function, and cognitive structuring and processing, the environment he creates, his affect on the ecosystem and his association with others of his kind and the planet we all live on. If you put him in a box, there's no tellin' what's gonna pop out when you turn his crank. Put a lion in an exhibit, and pretty soon after going in all those meaningless circles, he's not so much a lion any more. It's that simple. Removing man from his original habitat causes him to deteriorate in many ways. Going to brain science to deal with the social problems of our youth is to shift the blame from neglect and lack of sound parenting from mature adults, to genes and chemicals or neural dysfunction. Now it's all God's fault. This is all a result of rationalization and a fantasy generated to make you think it's something other than the stark reality of the social annihilation that has been happening in our society. Individuals don't have what they need to face the level of their selfishness. So the pharmaceutical companies play the same role as the churches, they have a remedy to "*keep you going and satisfied in an irreligious system*" The parent can even be concerned about his son's erratic behavior but not find the solution on the menu of options provided by society. The doc comes back with pictures of his son's brain and explanations about neural activity in certain regions, and then some drugs that can maybe make the brain do different stuff, (which further alienates the child). But the parent isn't educated to be able to even hear the voice of his conscience in this matter for lack of options. The parent is expected to conform to a system that's actually the biggest part of the problem of what is wrong with little Jimmy. Positivism seems to thwart the finger of blame from the modern industrial technosocieties's psychological impact on "the people", and places the blame on those afflicted. Opportunity for legitimate order to enslave.

Two primary pathways to onset:

- <u>Primary onset by liberation-</u> the process of rational development where you are exercising liberties granted, or attained. The release of accountability for behavior, allows one to be demoralized unknowingly behind closed doors. Rate of progression can range from slow desensitization over time, to single affectual action. Homeostasis was initially a group coordination and effort. This was part of them having a strong spirit that thrived, with a strong moral force in lifestyle. Individual homeostasis is alien to social creatures, and so by its essence is all deviance of social and psychological well being.

- <u>Secondary onset by exposure-</u> primary liberation pathway creates secondary pathway by exposure. This leads to secondary variant types. Conflict occurs psychologically creating the pathway to psychopathy (*suffering of the soul*) by direct emotional and psychological impact from being subject to apathy. Its construct is all social rationality process in response to being exposed to sociopathy. This includes exposure by proxy- that is a rational process that leads to both primary and secondary types, generating an anti-socialization that deprives healthy social development. This would be the process of rational development while internalizing antisocial norms in adaptation to industrialization, corporatism, institutionalization, politics, and religion.

     i. variants

When the process went on-set for the general population during the 50's, Social Psychologist Erich Fromm detected a sickness in modern society. In his book called Sane Society, he explains in *"normative humanism"* observations, a narcissism in society, explaining that it's actually a normal state for a certain period of childhood development, but now exists in later stages of life called *"secondary narcissism"* according to Freud- *"if the child fails to develop the capacity for love, or loses it again."* Then he adds *"Narcissism is the essence of all severe psychic pathology. For the narcissistically involved person, there is only one reality, that of his own thought."* [page 35] The words *"essense of all severe psychic pathology"* leaves a strong indication of a cumulative feature, and an opening door to other stages unknown. The explosion of mental illness in society is a direct consequence of losing our family structure, which quickly brought about two decades of deranged psychopathic serial killers. All that has happened since the beginning of our golden age -all the corruption and demoralization- was all the symptoms of sociopathy in process. A sociopath or psychopath is simply a completely demoralized soul. But it's been all a part of excelling the democratic society to rise to absolute reign of the world, and sociopathy is how that system rises to reign so quickly and absolutely.

Macro- you have all the sociopathic types in the specific functions in the stratus; from the simple common folk with their carrot to turn the millstone, to the primary interpersonal overachievers reaping in the wealth of the nations, with their violent psychopathic counter types to spill blood- even two-bit thugs for the industries who employ them in underground dwellings, who bring in money under the table as they exploit the opportunity afforded by the vulnerable ones beneath the cracks. So it's all very pragmatic and practical in its rationality, but not so conducive to a moral standard of a collective conscience that's only applicable to meet the common ends; all serving to sustain all. Fromm paints a picture with his observations of the environment in society, that I consider to be the perfect breeding ground for sociopathic pathogens, each using others for self interests; *"What is modern man's relationship to his fellow man? It is one between two abstractions, two living machines, who use each other. The employer uses the ones whom he employs; the salesman uses his customers. Everybody is to everybody else a commodity, always to be treated with certain friendliness, because even if he is not of use now, he may be later. There is not much love or hate to be found in human relations of our day. There is, rather, a superficial friendliness, and a more than superficial fairness, but behind the surface is distance and indifference."* [Fromm page 138-139]

In the circumspect of this theory, I consider this writing from Erich Fromm to be a documentation of the onset of sociopathy in the general population in 1955, starting with those who revert to narcissistic stage of development in adulthood -*"secondary narcissism"*. First depicted by Freud as those who had once learned the capacity to love, but then lost it. Initiating onset by the release of dependence on others, that begins a *social neurosis* that gradually deteriorates all social existence within all spheres of society, losing ability to maintain healthy relationships whether family or friend or even fellow man. By the third or fourth generation from initial onset, you end up with an entire generation of sociopaths   In our case, onset at the beginning of the roaring 20s with the infection of materialistic values in social networks, and within the general population by the 50s. Over time, their materialistic values would supersede their importance for each other. This is what brought a collapse of family structure, and by the seventies, we were entering into sociopathic lifestyles; with the drug freaks, the sexual sociopaths in the disco venues, and psychopathic killers like hard-core biker gangs who were extremely violent. Beginning with the initial documentation of the condition at the end of the 20s. George E. Partridge's observation of the condition he called sociopathy will be the definition of the term in response to the DSM, "*anything deviated or pathological in social relations*". The term Psychopathy that occurs later, is a reference to the counter type and the context of the term will be as it's original definition of the word psychopath; "suffering soul." Psychopathy is just the second level of the condition of sociopathy that creates violent counter types. This condition was documented by J.L.A. Koch in Europe during the 19th century where societies had already been on different levels of progression. U.S.A. has been on its own stage of the progression.

Humanistic observations in response to the Diagnostic Statistical Manual III:
Sociopathy: Initial onset pathway- liberation

NPI & NPII - DSM III Raskin & Terry 1988 established seven narcissistic factors - Authority, Exhibitionism, Superiority, Entitlement,/ Exploitativeness, Self Sufficiency, and Vanity NPI is known as the primary and represents the first 4 factors, NPII is secondary and includes the remaining 3 factors.

Humanist observation- NPI is normal for toddler years where boundaries are established to begin social development of learning the capacity to love. Blank-slates are those that did not achieve this capacity. They will not experience the process of desensitization and awakening. They are in an operational mode that was developed through the strivings under restraint. They do not understand emotions, and don't know how to have the appropriate response. Though they will simulate emotions to manipulate, or hide their deficit.

NPII would initially be a consequence of reverting by liberation after development. Simple point of being liberated from subjectivity, breaks down the social construct of reality as to the definitions they put on actions without giving account to external check and balance. This is where the rational mind of the individual forsakes his spirit, and now only seeks to stimulate the senses rather than meet the moral obligation of the collective conscience. At this point, there seems to be an affectual detachment to ease the cognitive dissonance. Characteristics become more pronounced, as affect is desensitized, and social rationality more compound and intellectual. This would represent the construct of sociopathy. Upon liberation, they return to primary NPI, and immediately develop the characteristics of exploitation, and in removing their account to others, learn to be self-sufficient by manipulation. This causes them to return to L2 limbic cycling of toddler years, that involves preoccupation with stimuli. When all is obtained from their own efforts, they only have themselves to adore and appreciate. Vanity is just self achievement.

Internal operation- In the instance of an emotional dilemma, their lack of spontaneous emotion leaves them to grope about in their critical and problem solving cognitive processes at the right posterior *VLPFC (BA 45)*, in uncertain decisions, access ethical memory for an appropriate response, rather than sudden spontaneous emotional release. The ethical responses generally conflict with moral emotional thresholds, and violate their norms. *"particularly conning and manipulative individuals showing reduced activity in the entire moral neural circuit."* Once the cognitive groping finds a reasonably suitable response, this response becomes automatic when the occasion arises. This routine developed from lack of affect in decisions, causes the PCC to develop a premature default mode (DFM) that usually occurs during elderly years.

Hypothesis on HPA- The substantive rationality to find consistency during adaptation desensitizes conscience and diminishes moral force to consider others in interpersonal affairs. This is what creates the secondary pathway, exposure by proxy. This pathway includes adaptation to lifestyle and environment created by sociopathic establishmentarianism. *"The hypothalamic – pituitary – adrenal (HPA) axis is essential for adaptation to environmental or homeostatic challenge. Activation of the HPA axis is controlled by neurons of the hypothalamic paraventricular nucleus (PVN), which coordinate responses to real or perceived threats to homeostasis."* It is in one's own pursuit, that they tolerate betraying the common conscience to love, in order to adapt to self sufficiency. Homeostasis should not include a process of competing and striving against, taxing, exploiting the welfare of others in acquisition, and especially ignoring vital needs of others. To the common conscience it is supposed to be a process of combining resources and efforts in taking care of all. If corporate CEO's have a propensity to apathetically exploit others, this ethic will carry down the corporate ladder for others to adapt to. This pathway is a gradual rate of progression.

Mechanical disengagement of spiritual function- the sensory of spirit at the amygdala depends on proper communication between the amygdala and certain lobes throughout the cerebral cortex for this function of love. Damaging the prefrontal cortex disables this connection and function with the moral force of spirit. *"During the past centuries, several researchers have described that there are personality changes that occurred after frontal lobe injuries. One of the most important cases was about Phineas Gage, who was a gentle, polite, sociable young man until a large iron rod went through his eye-damaging his prefrontal cortex. This injury made him emotionally insensitive, perform socially inappropriate behaviors, and was unable to make a rational judgment. A recent study suggests that when there is damage to the prefrontal cortex, there are five sub-types of personality changes that occur, and these include: Executive disturbances, Disturbed social behavior, Emotional Dysregulation, Hypo- emotionality/de energization, Distress, Decision making. The ability to decide involves reasoning, learning, and creativity"* [Physiology, Cerebral Cortex Functions by Khalid H. Jawabri; Sandeep Sharma]. The disorientation from this disconnect would result in the soul being put to sleep. So in the spiritual sense, it is more like Mr. Gage already died, and his body left on autopilot. This is where one becomes an automaton by mechanical breakdown. *"Following his recovery, an early observation of a change in Gage's personality was noted by Dr. John Harlow"*

Psychopathy: pathway- exposure

Lilienfield & Andrews 1996   PPI List of factors: egocentricity, social potency, cold heartedness PPII list of factors: care free non planfulness, fearlessness, blame externalization, impulsive nonconformity and stress immunity.

Humanist observation- Character typification: antisocial - probable case of blank-slate. Signs of neglect resulting in dichotomy of pathways. Neglect is a liberation by proxy, which is exposure to a sociopathic lifestyle. This results in deficits such as the ability to plan your day, or your tasks which are generally established through parenting. These things had to be put into a child. They don't come through a balance of brain chemistry. Cooperative development begins at toddler stage. To be healthy and not latent, they must learn during this time to not violate the other toddlers, but be able to play in the same room with them, and not violate their space, and take toys that don't belong to them. Contentment with what one has and the space given to them must be achieved to begin social development.   They must learn emotional boundaries by the time the oedipus stage begins between 4 and 6 years old. This is where social development can begin if emotional need was achieved during toddler years. If this is not achieved early enough, they will lack the social development to have an adequate complexity to cognitive structure that comes about through social networking. This is where they become hyper rational, for lack of cognitive accountability. There has to be adequate parental involvement to keep their rational mind in check, and snap them out of their fantasy that they aren't being mean to their little sister when they are. And they must suffer a consequence for their behavior by the loving parent that strives to establish this moral force of conscience. This is where the spirit is planted in our soul by the commands of love by those who love us. This is how spirit procreates in the souls of man and woman. This can happen late in life by family of choice if not achieved by selection. But the soul has to be a recipient. They have to by choice choose to receive the command to love. They have to want to love after feeling ashamed of their selfishness.

LPS - (Levenson et al, 1994) Determined primary and secondary counter types. LPS - P primary subscale LPS - S secondary subscale.

Humanist Observation- operational definition: operation is still yet to be fully defined as to the pathways relating to counter types- type I by liberation, and type II by exposure.

BIS/BAS (Carver & White 1994). Composed a twenty item report that included three sub scales, Drive, Reward Responsiveness, and fun seeking.

Humanist observation- fun seeking consistent with a premature liberation by exposure pathway to onset- a fancy way of saying neglect. Reward Responsiveness- this type by the characteristics had become a norm for lack of cooperative development that brought some of the indoctrination from idealists' with alternatives to the consequence of spanking. These ideologies, like Dr. Spock's, resulted in forms of bribery with mechanisms of stimuli used as motivators to control behavior. Humanist observation found this approach turns them into manipulators. These types are generally left to these mechanisms that are primarily composed of their fun seeking. Child is not being directed towards healthy ambitions, and the alternatives remove the child's need of learning the consequence for their actions. Lack of sound moral programming and critical cognitive development. They need a will from a loving father who will see their development through. Independence has removed that. So spanking becomes abusive when there is no investment of love in them, and you're just trying to manipulate them.

AQ (Aggression Questionnaire)   Bus & Perry 1992 List of factors: physical aggression, verbal aggression, anger, hostility.

Humanist observation- Characteristic typification: LPS -S secondary subtype, anxiety driven. This would be in the category of psychopath, hence the suffering of the soul. Primary pathway for this would be exposure, and or exposure by proxy. This variable is the advanced consequence of children not getting social needs. There is a probability that this variable has much to do with a high level of exposure causing various forms of trauma. A toddler not supervised can slowly become a monster without others realizing the levels of his violation involving the other children. Even biting, hair pulling, and face scratching to get their way. The chance they have is in this time where they are in need of supervision with correction and discipline. This is probably the most important time for investment, and the most common time these days of being overlooked and left with mechanisms of intrigue and preoccupation.

Anger generally linked to emotional trauma, leaving them in a livid state; type of anger from being bruised. Significant desensitization of Affect which can go all the way if brutality had diminished whatever thresholds there might have been in sensitivity. Some of these outbursts can be a probable indication of moral indignation, which given the circumstance could be a normal emotional response. Emotional outburst results in high frequencies of activity in moral regions. This would indicate some moral force still remaining. Though moral programming is generally reversed.   This would indicate an abused spirit, with a possibility of restoring affectual sensitivity if given the right care and investment in them starting with the tenets of Trauma Informed Care with an empathy strengths based approach.   General plight of this, is the amount of investment would be life demanding, and only a few would be able to be restored affectually. They needed a family to bring them healing. There is a point where you know by sincere investment, that there is no chance of recovery. Institutions with their white coats treat them like subjects that condescend in ways that are cruel. This can trigger old wounds that are deep and agonizing. So they can lash out violently and not feel guilty because in that moment, they are the victim, who is generally criminalized for their choice of coping with the devastation of their life. So those who are examining them are all just part of the nightmare they are trying to escape with their coping mechanisms. So the white coats are like monsters in their nightmare.

When ptsd and complex trauma is being afflicted on a child, the hope is that it is not too excessive, and that reprocessing with CBT and CEBT comes soon enough. If they are a type two that revert, then they can maybe get help. Once Affect is desensitized, there's no healing that can come by therapy. They're an emotional flat-line; spiritually deceased.

(PDQ - R Hyler & rieder 1987). Personality Diagnostic Questionnaire - Revised The Borderline subscale questionnaire assesses borderline personality traits based on the criteria noted in the Diagnostic Statistical Manual DSM III American Psychiatric Association. 1980

Humanist observation- In my experience with many cases, Borderlines fit into this secondary subtype. Common affinity is they all suffer from abandonment. If this occurs before conscience is established, they are a blankslate. If after, emotionally they suffer tremendously, and are in need of life demanding investment to heal and restore them from their latency in development. To a true humanist, we see that approaching someone's personal pain with a clinical or institutional approach has a psychological impact that only further compounds the complexities of their trauma. So this would be similar to how the *Hawthorne Effect* influences the research if the person being examined is under the perception conveyed by these deficit oriented approaches to their social tendencies to violate- it is a negative feed to their internal oppression. This would have a negative effect on the likert scale self evaluation analysis. I've experienced this working in institutions voluntarily to help the afflicted, I myself being one of them. The actual violations in the institutions were the result of institutional cruelty, but had an impact on the subject's internal oppression, that they were at fault. This phenomenon was discovered and researched by Philip Hallie. HIs work determined that there was a dehumanizing cruelty going unchecked within the institutions, and stated this cruelty demotes individuality. Hallie sited a quote from a Nazi SS Officer stating, "Commitment to an institution that overrides all sentimentality transforms cruelty and destruction into moral nobility, and commitment is the lifeblood of an institution." (Hallie "From Cruelty to Goodness" 7).

Definition- So to clarify as for the purpose of this recontextualization, a "*sociopath*" could include all six of the clusters of variants documented in the DSM, but a "*psychopath*", would be a reference to the two types who are violent and unstable. All variants are sociopathic, and the psychopath is a reference to the secondary type of sociopaths who are violent and driven by anxiety. These types are known to suffer tremendously psychologically. Secondary violent types are primarily in the pathway by exposure, and suffer profuse levels of trauma. Studies have logged variants as a "construct". My observations have come to the conclusion of a destruct rather than a "construct" when it comes to affectual sensitivity. The part of the condition that would represent any level of construct, would be that of the rational development.

Analysis- Sociopathy starts with the initial onset of secondary narcissism in the pathway by liberation, that produce -by exposure- the secondary subtypes. Secondary narcissists produce blank slates, who remain in primary narcissism, never learning to love. All the variants logged in the Diagnostic Statistical Manual are all part of the same condition that I simply refer to as 'sociopathy' ("*anything deviated or pathological in social relations" George E. Partridge*). These stages of its development also have attributes that differ according to personal characteristics, genetics, situational and environmental influences. It can also be brutally killing someone for selfish gain, which I consider to be in the realm of psychopathy; a variant category exhibiting psychological disturbances resulting in suffering of the soul. These sufferings involve confusions about God and world perspectives, and moral isolation from the confusion in moral programing resulting in a complex of factors of emotional instabilities that destroy their attempts at social networking.   The Limbic system destabilizes and desperation to survive exceeds levels of resiliency. A primary type can be enjoying his exploitation of others, whereas a psychopath is in mental torment. Psychopath literally means "*suffering soul*" [J.L.A. Koch 1888].

So toleration for behavior sways with the progression over time, and sociopathy is now not so much considered a problematic illness in capitalistic society. In fact, sociopaths helped to advance capitalism to the pinnacle of its achievement. What I found very interesting was that Fromm referred to greed as insanity, which is a typical sociopathic characteristic that can get to the point of a tortured mind given the right conditions. Mister smooth talker might not be so composed if he suddenly found himself robbed of all his cunningly acquired wealth.   These fine clad CEOs would likely become a salivating animal on a murderous rampage. Or just blow their brains out.   Either way, their condition would be abundantly clear to all. Even now, madness can be seen in the faces of political leaders who are being tested by fire.

Villains like Jack the Ripper and Jeffrey Dahmer have no concept of what a human being is. They see material and nothing else. This can be attributed to the commodification of man; things to use for self interests. Once affective sense is gone, we're left at the mercy of their flesh and its demands. An interesting correlation is in the time duration from the initial industrial revolution of both England and America. A century after England's industrial revolution, Jack the Ripper lurks the streets with a disturbing level of the condition that involves a dissecting complex. Approximately a century later after America's industrial revolution, Jeffrey Dahmer lurks the streets with the same disturbing level of the condition, also having a dissecting disorder. Both represent an extreme level of progression in their liberated society. But unlike Jack the Ripper, who we know almost nothing about, Jeffery Dahmer gave us some insight as to the contributing factors, and the suffering of his soul. He was the son of a forensic pathologist, and was immediately exposed to the reality of death. Cadavers were something of a norm in his childhood. But most of his childhood was an isolated experience left alone with a mentally ill mother. Adolescence brought impulses and curiosities that lead to dissecting neighborhood pets. His rational mind developed a very high level of intelligence. But one thing notable was his deep need for companionship. Moral isolation combined with physical isolation becomes unbearable (Fromm 1955). By the time of adulthood, he would invite people over to his house for a nice visit, but the problem was they would go to leave. He explained this to be the motive for killing his victims and keeping their body parts, he didn't want them to leave.

> Relatedness vs. narcissism- *"Even if all his physiological needs were satisfied, he would experience his state of aloneness and individuation as a prison from which he had to break out in order to retain his sanity. In fact, the insane person is the one who has completely failed to establish any kind of union, and is imprisoned, even if he is not behind barred windows. The necessity to unite with other living beings, to be related to them, is an imperative need on the fulfillment of which man's sanity depends."* [Sane Society, pg 30] This is the ultimate destiny of individualism.

Empirical Correlation- There was the only time I saw emotion on Dahmer's face for his actions, and that was when he was explaining how he coped with them by telling himself they weren't really people, but that they were just things. The interviewer answered with "and that made it easier for you?" Then Dahmer answered yes and choked up for a moment, and quickly stopped as if his rational mind was voluntarily and knowingly creating a detachment of Affect by rational fantasy to escape the horror of reality. He even looks down and to the side during the emotion which would indicate type of cognition. This is a significant correlation that demonstrates the rational construct in the process of desensitization by executive order. What he needed was someone to keep his rational mind in check when he was growing up. He had social needs that society generally doesn't provide. And so we end up with bad combinations. Another is Son of Sam. His rampage began after he discovered mom didn't really die, but abandoned him.

Neurology- *"Negative association between psychopathy and brain activity during emotional moral decision-making. (Left) Higher total psychopathy scores (and all factors of psychopathy) were associated with reduced left amygdala activity (−21, −10, −14; 98 voxels, T=3.32, P=0.011, corrected). (Middle) Factors of psychopathy. (Right) The interpersonal factor was also associated with reduced activity in medial prefrontal cortex (−4, 60, 14; 98 voxels, T=2.67, P=0.030, corrected), posterior cingulate (0, −66, 35; 14 voxels, T=2.01, P=0.037, corrected), and angular gyrus (56, −66, 24; 56 voxels, T=2.50, P=0.012, corrected). No positive associations were significant. Anatomical labels: AMG, amygdala; PCC, posterior cingulate; MPFC, medial prefrontal cortex; ANG, angular gyrus. [Published: 19 December 2008 The neural correlates of moral decision-making in psychopathy* [A L Glenn, A Raine, & R A Schug, Molecular Psychiatry volume 14, Pages 5–6(2009)Cite this article]

End of the Duel- When rationality has completely diminished Affect, in interpersonal interactions, lifestyle, and social relations, dualism ends its cycle between conscience and individual; the absolute completion of the process. Even the dismantling of family structure was part of reaching this level of individualization. It goes to destroy and individualize even households, so all members lack affection and are separated from each other with a mutual agreement to live separate lives. This is a spiritual disconnect of life force that we get in our true social existence. This contraction of family reduces individuals' perspective down to their own immediate network, and so this dwindles down the cognitive processing structure, so relatedness is replaced with the imaginary, and all value is only found within the boundaries of these inner worlds. Ego only emerged when collective identity was lost.

The ego is an appendage from all esteem only being left to self achievement, which then becomes worthless because man's true worth is only found in seeing internally and mechanically his importance to his clan, and their importance to him. Proper esteem of others only occurs within a small common life society, with an exchange of dependence on each other. Now we have others to appreciate because they are all part of our achievement, and we a part of theirs. This is of greater value than that of just individuals. Structure has a role of indoctrinating individual perspective through propaganda, and curriculums designed for individual independent society that leave no escape route from your private cell. Freudian Orthodoxy was a concise set of guidelines for life in the modern world that applies to all areas of *"individual existence- interpersonal relations of all sorts, child rearing, attitudes to occupation and careers, all varieties of private things, hobbies, religion,"* [Berger & Kellner].

Four correlating factors of sociopathy:

- **Affective**- *(i.e., lack of remorse or guilt, shallow affect, callous/lack of empathy, failure to accept responsibility for own actions).* Affective onset can occur within any of the two pathways in society. This is where initial onset occurs starting from a rationalization during a transvaluation of values in the strife to find consistency to relieve discomfort of guilt communicated from the spirit within the soul. Should be of greatest concern, that a person would harm others without feeling bad about it. Seems to guarantee probability of further offenses, little hope in restitution. Leaves a frightening question as to the capacity of what a person is capable of without this sensitivity. Almost like something had died in them, or someone.

- **Interpersonal**- *(i.e., glibness/superficial charm, grandiose sense of self-worth, pathological lying, cunning/manipulative).* Society seems to have all the motivators to generate these personality traits: there's an expectation to be charming, because the entire system demands the "*market character*" to survive (Fromm 1955). As he documented in *Sane Society*, it doesn't depend on your ability to do the job, it depends on your ability to sell a favorable personality. Both church and politics function on those who have very grandiose types of characters. They all come as to be the big hero who's gonna fix everything, and boast of their greatness. Everyone seems to go to them because they have all the success, but it's all stockpiled for themselves. They have the most, and demand the most say-so. They say that not voting them in to be in control is to not do your part for your nation, and is irresponsible. In reality, those voting them in are ordaining the most selfish to be in control of our welfare, and domestic prosperity. As far as pathological lying. It also seems to be the norm in the general spheres of society. You're even expected to fudge everything about your history to get jobs, politicians lying and not making good on promises made in campaign is tolerated,,,even expected. It is a system based on the paradigm of self interests, and your problem is not my problem. This seems to be the general attitude of citizens, who are astounded when politicians tell them in so many words 'your problem is not my problem'.

About manipulation, individual independence results in the commodification of people in society, leaving us with the only conclusion; that to achieve i must be cunning and manipulative. The most cunning manipulators become the most successful and dominating in an individualistic society. Both church and state. This is the consequence of removing dependence, and the instigation to forced adaptation.

- **Lifestyle**- *(i.e., need for stimulation/proneness to boredom, parasitic lifestyle, lack of realistic long-term goals, impulsivity, irresponsibility)* Traditional and value rationalization is a significant influence on this variable. The breakdown of cooperation really is a consequence of the breakdown of mechanical solidarity under a common interest within a collective. Separate interests send us in different directions. So this factor would be a result of exposure to forced adaptation to self sufficiency. Responsibility is developed during adolescence when they are learning to be liberated as an individual.

  This is established by careful observance of behavior under liberation, and correction as they develop, earning more and more responsibilities that are represented by the Father and Mother figures. The roots of this begins with the hopes of preadolescents to be a "big boy". The results of their responsibility can't be left to the imagination. They must see this mechanically within their group, or the meaning is lost with the aspirations to fuel the growth of maturity. This all depends on a trust that they have developed, a progression over time while being with you in their private personal situations. This is what was removed when independence had to establish institutions to deal with the 'kids', when there is no collective community. A consequence of true social networking breaking down in the attempt to create a synthetic organic solidarity. The organics that depend on differences are only supposed to exist between the ecological system and man, not between man and man. Social void arouses a need to stimulate.

- **Antisocial**- *(i.e., poor behavioral controls, early behavior problems, juvenile delinquency, revocation of conditional release, criminal versatility).* This is a result of children simply being denied their social development.

Man without his spirit just becomes a creature of instinct, programmed for stimulation and materialistic consumption.

It's quite evident in my experience that the general population in the 80's slipped into complacency; a pre-conscience confidence in the sociopathic lifestyle. Precontemplation is due to the lack of subjectivity to others. This is where individual perspective is locked in, and where cognitive dissonance has ceased, because conscience is no longer communicating either by desensitization, or blank slate.. No sharing of private life, leaves no one to snap you out of it. Contemplation is an awakening to the problem, but involves a groping as to the solution. This would need "*real circumstance*", for "*real consequence*", or process starts all over again, returning to the problem with a different perspective and method, but still in need of real solution. Chance for another awakening is even more difficult and complicated, especially if an undesirable coping mechanism is replaced with another more tolerable one. Likelihood of denial is very high, for protective reasons. There are many acts of violence, and even killings that are generated by the confusion of the individual perspective which misses most of what's really going on, and is left to the imagination to fill in the blanks. A person can even experience terror from the things in their imagination, that aren't the actual facts of the situation. This is why I implement sociological perspective with psychotherapy.

ii. pathogens

Operation and construct of sociopathy- I profess that it was Max Weber who discovered and documented the operation and construct of sociopathy, the term given by George E. Partridge only 8 years after Max Weber's Economy and Society was published. Partridge was documenting the condition that resulted from the rationalization. In my observation of the social action rationalities and the process of their development, I noticed the thoughts they conjure correlate to pathogens that can spawn rapidly and can infect others by contact. The deliberation of the rational mind can spawn new thoughts in microseconds, that can even be contracted from a host who can infect everyone in the environment. Only a few have a strong immune system of moral value. These infestations are induced by external influences and the forces of interests in "*affinities, antagonisms, and sociological anchorings.*" Excerpt- "*A central feature of Weber's sociology was his belief that sociological inquiry should be grounded in the analysis of how individuals attach "meanings" to their "social actions.""* It is in these "meanings" attached to social actions that we can detect pathogens.

In a journal report called *THE CRIMINAL PSYCHOPATH*, researchers referred to the mind of a psychopath as "hyper-rational", and connote their rational mind as the determining factor in their behavior; *"78 Once we recognize that the key to criminal responsibility is rationality, and a sufficiently rich kind of rationality not only to navigate the perceived world but also to perceive it with reasonable accuracy, then what about psychopaths? They are certainly rational in the narrow sense of being able to determine their best interest and to navigate in the world to achieve that interest. In fact, in some sense they are hyper-rational."* [Jurimetrics. 2011 Summer; 51: 355–397. Kent A. Kiehl and Morris B. Hoffman]

Rationality and Social Action- In Weber's view, social actions could be classified into four types: "instrumentally rational (zweckrational)," "value-rational (wertrational)," "affectual," and "traditional," though he noted that this list was not necessarily "exhaustive" (E&S 1.1.2).

- *A traditional action was one that was habitual, which meant that, while it might be meaningful, it was done more out of routine than any conscious deliberation.*
- *An affectual action was one undertaken as a means of satisfying the immediate demands of an emotional state, such as romantic passion or anger. Like traditional action, affectual action did not arise from deliberation.*
- *A value-rational action was one taken out of the self-conscious conviction that the action has a value inherent to itself, independent of any outcome it might or might not have.*
- *Finally, an instrumentally rational action was one taken based on its anticipated ability to achieve some considered end (Zweck, in German)."* [James Schmidt March 7, 2015]

Define and categorize pathways to rationalities- so if we take these 4 social action rationalities, and apply them to the 4 pathways -liberation, exposure, anti socialization, and single act- in the chronology of the progression in the hypothesis, we can see some of the actual operation.

Liberation- pathway to sociopathy onset: process of rational development where you are exercising liberties granted or attained while released from subjectivity. This would arouse and engage in deliberating a social action also by value, and or means-end rationality. All this is part of the initiation into a newly acquired lifestyle granted by the opportunities in being liberated from critical thought. This would also arouse and engage in affectual rationality in moments of unexpected opportunity, which is enveloped by either *value* or *instrumental* rationality, (also known as "means-end"), *"An affectual action was one undertaken as a means of satisfying the immediate demands of an emotional state, such as romantic passion or anger. Like traditional action, affectual action did not arise from deliberation".* Sociopathy was discovered when liberated people were relieving the immediate demands of an emotional state after a sexual revolution developed the demand to stimulate. A killing can also be the result of relieving the demands of an emotional state. In this pathway it would be by opportunity of acquiring something valued. Pathogens- Cognitive dissonance would come after violation, with a theoretical rationale remedy to relieve the feelings of guilt. Unsubstantiated needs is the typical modus operandi for pathogens; "fun is a need" postulate "it helps me cope ". The cooperation with the narcissistic pursuit is the role of the pathogen, to delegate the action according to the value constellations that constitute the acquired "way of life".

"Rationalization processes of historic significance in societies, and in entire civilizations, have often originated when a constellation of factors crystallized that rewarded methodical rational ways of life."

Man develops rationality as he exchanges values as motivators- *"In sociology, rationalization (or rationalisation) is the replacement of traditions, values, and emotions as motivators for behavior in society with concepts based on rationality and reason"* (Giddens,2013).

Rationalization is the process of a *"transvaluation of values"* (Neitzche), that infects our entire being which determines social health and domestic prosperity. It's really the independence that allows for this rationalization to emerge and go unchecked. It depends on the individual to hold himself accountable, or be the one to choose who's going to tell him what he needs to hear to confirm the inner voice. Man has built a fortress to guard from this sort of subjectivity. Without his clan who knows him from a tot, he has no point of reference. True reality cannot be discovered without an interdependency. Reality is where our guilt lies that sickens the spirit, and we can't find the remedy in our fantasy. The individual is trapped in this state. It takes a trusting, a certain level of deference, with the right motive to really be able to find it, and it's discovery is painful and difficult to receive. Sociopathy is the conclusion of a conflict of values between the collective conscious spirit, and the selfish will of the individual. Our rational development is an addendum generated by this conflict of values.

Ancient Rome- It all begins with domination; that is how the democratic structure is established by hegemony. Even the great philosophers who were the architects appealed to the wealthy with their mastery ideas. So the process really starts with them conquering and dominating with formal rationalization: *A "rational" form of lawmaking, for example, did not originate in those countries that first introduced modern forms of capitalism. Instead, it arose and attained a highly rationalized form in ancient Rome. It was taken over in the Catholic countries of southern Europe long before the onset of industrialization in that area rather than by England, the earliest country to industrialize." [Stephen Kalberg The American Journal of Sociology, Vol. 85, No. 5 (Mar., 1980), pp. 1145-1179]*

To set the grounds for this domination, there has to be a theoretical rationality for permissive doctrines of clemency. *"With the appearance of ethical salvation religions, ethical priests, monks, and theologians rationalized the values implicit in doctrines into internally consistent constellations of values, or world views (Weltbilder), that offered comprehensive explanations for the perpetuation of suffering." (Mar., 1980)* These doctrines are full of pathogens to justify actions against the moral voice within, and explain their inconsistencies with ethically prescribed orders of ritual for propitiation. Theoretical confrontation with reality to introduce new regularities to place meanings on actions that alter affective attitude. Rational fantasy enters complacency. Affectual sensory remains impaired as long as the spell goes unbroken. Fantasy grows as this compounds, new rationalities for new inconsistencies with ethical ritual for propitiation.

So this is the role that the churches played in the process of sociopathy within democratic societies. In 1 Tim 4:2, it is written that false teachings come from hypocritical liars who have seared their conscience as with a hot iron, which one could imagine killing all the nerve endings so as to lose all feeling and sensitivity. This would suggest that lying was part of their conscience being seared. Probable likelihood of false teachings that were permissive doctrines to excuse one of behavior condemned by the conscience. 2 Tim 3:1-5 is a prophesy of how the church in the end times would produce sociopaths, even giving detailed examples of behavior that correspond to the four correlating factors logged in the DSM; *"But mark this: There will be terrible times in the last days. People will be lovers of themselves, lovers of money, boastful, proud, abusive, disobedient to their parents, ungrateful, unholy, without love, unforgiving, slanderous, without self-control, brutal, not lovers of the good, treacherous, rash, conceited, lovers of pleasure rather than lovers of God— having a form of godliness but denying its power. Have nothing to do with such people"*. There's certain things that leaders of churches would do that revealed sociopathic behavior. Those led by such teachings were self condemned by the denial of the truth when it came to them by messenger.

Ending the inner wrestling- Page 216, Fromm responds to Durkheim; *"the individual and the group have ceased to function satisfactorily, they live in a condition of "amonie", that is, a lack of meaningful and structurealized social life. This individual, free from all genuine social bonds, finds himself abandoned, isolated, and demoralized."* [1955] If we look at what Fromm was saying here, he essentially was stating in fact that the release from social bonds leads to demoralization. Fromm was trying to warn us of the complete demoralization of our society, and it came quickly, and on a level no one expected. After the release from subjectivity, those who initially had a conscience eventually gave up the dual, by 'letting go of the guilt'. It is still retaining some level of moral value that causes us to continue the dual, that is unlikely to survive today's standard of expectations in society. It seems quite easy to understand; decrease in sensitivity of conscience, is in direct correlation to social breakdown and increase of crime in all forms, even crimes committed by law makers and enforcers, and world leaders with acts of cruelty by opportunism. Sociopathy isn't limited to the confines of those who have no conscience at all, it is a terminal condition of the spirit and soul that has only one antidote; Word of God who is love from another soul that comes with a small voice that presents itself with the moral obligation of confession and repentance.

Exposure- pathway to psychopathy onset: pathogens contracted while being exposed to sociopathic behavior; abuse, violation, rejection, exploitation, estrangement, neglect, post traumatic stress and complex trauma, where sometimes you lose moral identity and development in the confusion. This is the next stage of social neurosis, that goes right to the breakdown of cognitive structuring, that leads to wellbeing. This is where suffering of the soul begins because of various deficits in development. Neglect alone can cause severe levels of suffering in the soul given the rate. This pathway leads to its own form of blank-slate. Both primary and secondary blank-slates have conditioned behaviors and propensities given the influences and forces within the exposure environment.

Affectual Rationality to Exposure- Emotional trauma creates emotional instability when on a certain level. Emotional instability leaves us shut out of vital networks. You feel criminalized for just trying to survive, and discarded by society who oppresses you, which greatly increases the severity of their plight. Desperation reaches intense levels, and actions that violate conscience often come after these intense situations when returning from L1, or an instance of L2. Internal oppression develops from the confusion of why they react. This force within is like a tyrant over them, beating them over and over. It is in the levels of this form of suffering that can totally desensitize the Affect. For the most severe levels of trauma, they lack necessary interaction from absence of network, sometimes so bad that they slip into a place where there's no cognitive confirmation of reality. This makes them prime to fall into the imaginary. Psychopathy is a reaction to exposure to sociopathic behavior that causes psychological sufferings that reach for mechanisms of escape. The imaginary just happens to be your only route of escape. These sufferings involve fretting and even reliving moments of terror that can haunt them even daily. They lack adequate cognitive processing structure to limit boundaries of fantasy, and confirm a healthy reality in which one wants to exist.

Psychological trauma disrupts the processing, and leads to unbearable conclusions with no one to help you process. Envy and jealous rage can destroy a man within. Malice is to desire that others would suffer. This generally comes from suffering at the hands of others. A man's life can be destroyed in an instant in these societies of self-sufficiency. But these sufferings can simply exist within an individual perspective under a hyper-rational fantasy. In this exposure to sociopathic lifestyle, there is a breakdown in true social networking. This is paramount as to the leading cause of these internal sufferings due to lack of cognitive development. To someone who suffers from psychosis, the monsters in their illusions are real. They can suffer terror by the things simply conjured by a hyper-rational mind. Borderline cases seem to have a common attribute of a disruption in attachment form of ptsd, and it's ADD and bipolar type. By these findings, given expectations and the relative deficits, exposure to narcissism alone has the potential of producing borderline personality types.

Purpose in self leads to suicide- *"Durkheim warns us however that with the contraction of the family, individuality and the pursuit of purely individual goals have increased. When the individual "looks for his purpose within himself, he falls into a state of moral misery which leads him to suicide" (Marcuse 1975 [1892], p. 236)."* This seems to be the inevitable destiny of individual independence; it leads to mental illness and sufferings of the soul so deep, with suicide as the only hope of escape- to have to end their life. The bureaucratic rational mind closes all avenues of escaping the process, by enforcing self sufficiency.

Exposure by proxy- anti-socialization is a process of rational development while internalizing antisocial norms when giving in to the pressures to adapt to commodification, industrialization, corporatism, institutionalization, politics, and religion. *"How can conscience develop when the principle of life is conformity? Conscience, by its very nature, is nonconforming. It has to be* able to say "no". _To the degree to which a person conforms, he cannot hear the voice of his_ _conscience, much less act upon it._ Conscience only exists when man experiences himself as a man, not a thing, as a commodity." [Sane Society 1955]

I'm basing this pathway to onset by this quote, that suggests by its simple holistic concept, that conformity can completely remove the voice of our conscience. Industrial Psychology as a science in itself is a demonstration of socially educated man's concern about the psychological impact of working in the modern industrial workforce. Erich Fromm gives some examples of this impact. In his research he examined the "_socially patterned defect_", "_From the standpoint of_ _normative humanism we must arrive at a different concept of mental health; the very person who is considered healthy in the categories of an alienated world, from the humanistic stand-point appears as the sickest one-although not in terms of individual sickness, but of the_ _socially patterned defect. Mental health, in the humanistic sense, is characterized by the ability_ _to love and to create_".

He continues to give essentials of health -that it takes being able to "_emerge from the_ _ideas of infantile grandiosity into the conviction of ones real though limited strength_" to "_love life, and yet to accept death without terror; to tolerate uncertainty about the most important questions with which life confronts us -and yet to have faith in our thoughts and feelings, inasmuch as they are truly ours. To be able to be alone, and at the same time one with a loved person, with every brother on this earth, with all that is alive; to follow the voice of our_ _conscience, the voice that calls us to ourselves, yet not to indulge in self hate when the voice of conscience was not loud enough to be heard and followed. The mentally healthy person is the_ _person who lives by love, reason and faith, who respects life, his own and that of his fellow_ _man._" [pg 203 + 204].   On page 229, Fromm explains how the conscience is fettered by modern organization, in which we have to surmise would kill the spirit. A spirit cannot thrive under micromanagement. Somehow there has to be spontaneity in a freezone. Bondage and bounding break the spirit. It is like the mustangs, you can break their spirit so that they lose the desire for their purpose. All must be in cooperation with the initial intention of life, the very purpose for collective conscience.

The term "social norms" seems to be a misnomer in modern society. There should be a differentiation in what is "social norms", and what is "anti-social norms". There are anti-social perspectives and tendencies that have been creeping into our social networks, and creating norms. These influences play an essential role in the process of denying the things our conscience is trying to communicate. Fear of rejection and peer pressure can cause someone to do something they know is wrong, that they would never have done had it not been for the power of these forces. The norms of our society construct more of an anti-socialization. Actual socialization is almost non-existent in individual independent societies, where social norms are replaced with antisocial norms, until there are no more true social norms left. Society is a free for all, a mad frenzy to grab as much as you can in disregard of conscience for lack of being subject to others in need. This is a force contrary to the common conscience, which has a sense of moral obligation, one's fair share and providing for others, and being directly subject to those who don't have enough. Only when we yield and cooperate with this force within, does our soul remain healthy and our spirit awake.

Subject to individuals overriding critical standards- *"The intensity, the satisfaction and even the character of human needs, beyond the biological level, have always been preconditioned. Whether or not the possibility of doing or leaving, enjoying or destroying, possessing or rejecting something is seized as a need depends on whether or not it can be seen as desirable and necessary for the prevailing societal institutions and interests. In this sense, human needs are historical needs and, to the extent to which the society demands the repressive development of the individual, his needs themselves and their claim for satisfaction are subject to overriding critical standards. We may distinguish both true and false needs."* Erich Fromm explains how repulsive and disturbing habits in the economic strivings are poisoning the industries, which is expelled only by rearranging its scale of values. *"Economic functions involved in living, have inadvertently allowed pursuit to lead us into a condition of social disintegration that removes value and meaning to work."* [page 219] The original society didn't expose us to all these very powerful influences that are instrumental to the process of sociopathy. The structure of this society we find ourselves in, leaves us cut off from real social existence, to conform to external influences that are subject to change. Conscience is compromised in our adapting to norms foreign to the social creature man was created to be. As to support the adaptation factor; *"The conformity pattern develops a new morality, a new kind of superego. But the new morality is not the conscience of the humanistic tradition or is the new superego made in the image of an authoritarian father. Virtue is to be adjusted and to be like the rest. Vice, to be different."* [pg 158]

Here we can see how he's articulating just how man was replacing the old moral tradition, with a new one opposed to the conscience, but adequate for modern civilization. *"modern society consists of "atoms" (if we use the Greek equivalent of "individual"), little particles estranged from each other but held together by selfish interests and by the necessity to make use of each other." [page 140].* It is in this environment that we contract the disease that sickens, and gradually withers a man's soul as he goes about his business, so he becomes insensitive to others, an immoral creature whose behavior is not in the initial intention of life. He's not so concerned about the planet surviving his luxury and pleasure.

Single act- single act is the shortcut to the end. Conscience is usually slowly diminished to a dark level they never thought they would ever go. Single act would be going all the way and doing something such as killing another person as in the case with Cain and Abel. Cain was satisfying the immediate demand of jealous rage. This would involve affectual rationality and was the common pathway to those who suddenly became a sociopath within a collective. So the probable scenario would be that something had happened where it involved an affectual rationality. Either a case of value and or a means to an end. The headstrong individual with no collective conscience destroys community. They always have to be banished to spare the flock. This sickness can spread throughout the clan and turn them all into sociopaths by exposure.

.

Normal level of rationality in simple primitive means-end to appeasing a god- *"Against 19th-century French anthropology, Weber argued that man did not acquire his "rationality" with the Enlightenment and that individuals in all previous epochs were not incapable of rational action. On the con- trary, even everyday actions of "primitive" man could be subjectively means-end rational, as, for example, when specific religious rituals were performed with the aim of receiving favors from a god."* So the point isn't just rationality; there's certain tolerable levels for moral conscience. The point is an unconscious rational process not subject to critical standards, left to go wherever at will unrestrained. Though religious rituals were the result of rationality, there is also the religious action that is by faith- choosing to trust rather than have a practical rationality. The spirit is by faith, and it is implanted in our conscience and is spontaneous. Spirit knows the voice of the Father spirit, and the mind that heeds and cooperates is fulfilled. They simply love the voice of love. Religious ritual is for ignoring conscience, and is powerless to heal their sickened spirit by restoring their conscience.

Let us consider how the doctrine adjusts to the progression. When general populations were going into the black in the 70's with blatant acts of wickedness, the doctrine of salvation was adjusted to accommodate the new lifestyle and compromised to the point of 'anything goes, he died on the cross, so be as wicked as you want.' The ancient rituals acquired by practical rationality are not even used now. Any feeling of guilt is considered evil. Not even a century ago this would be ludicrous to the average christian. *"Churches belong to the conservative forces in society and use religion to keep man going and satisfied in an irreligious system. The religion will "degenerate into overt idolatry."*

Control by illusion- ancient motive for an illusion of collective unity. Being subject to the moral voice within can be hazardous to rulers and nobles. These representations and confrontations have to be abolished for *"anti-societal norms"* (Charles Darby) to be free to roam and rule. The history of roman democracy had a purpose for implementing syncretism for such an illusion of unity to avoid upheaval. It was a way of melding different schools of thought, and even religious concepts to obscure any differences. But it was a false sense of unity- an illusion. The more man has rationalized away his conscience, the more he has become estranged from his God and his fellow man. The more we're estranged, the more we have to use our imagination to have a sense of unity. But this all happens subconsciously.

It is a substantive rationalization process that we generate a fantasy to bring a sense of consistency, that this is all normal and ok, and that we're not being alienated and estranged from each other, when we really are. Fantasy increases with estrangement. Estrangement increases with apathy. The more we are apathetic, the more we are estranged, the more we are estranged, the more we are in a fantasy of unity. As long as there's tolerance, fantasy continues. What makes it difficult is the way society is spread out so far and complex in the way it functions. *"A society that's organization of people is too vast to be understood as a whole. Nothing can be seen in its totality."* [pg 170] So because our society is too vast and complex to observe, much goes on without us being able to grab a hold of what's really happening.

Determinations as far as a plan of action for a particular symptom are always just out of reach because of this obscurity. This leaves room for sociopaths to say "yeah, that's your theory", and so nothing substantial is ever done about anything. In modern society there is no real collective, because everyone is individualized. A collective conscience has the glutton of dependence in social life to sustain healthy spiritual function, and the sensitivity of conscience is of this paradigm. I don't even know if this society even has a collective awareness, because people aren't so much aware of each other. Collective conscience has a personal awareness and importance of each other, from a common life, also known as *"common conscious"* [Durkheim 1893]. Modern society seems to be having more of a collective fantasy, far removed from reality. It is simply that the general sense of identity has a common theme that attaches to the ego. This is what Erich Fromm was getting at with the two men in battle uniform; they risk their lives for each other because of their egos, instead of it being because they genuinely care for each other. It is an identity that is only connected to the ego, and not the true sense of real connection that comes from the collective, and so it is void of reality, and only exists in the imagination- image-nation. This is why the conscience has no "real consequence." *"If men define situations as real, they are real in their consequences."* [*Thomas Theory 1928*].

  "Imaginary"- rationality -free from all subjectivity- is a very dangerous combination of factors. Rationality can generate inner worlds of the imagination to create fantasy by which one puts himself and others that is not based in reality. As we are using our rationality to validate behavior contrary to the ultimate authority with opportunities afforded by the subordinate authority of man, we are producing false realities that accumulate fantasy that gradually increases in its boundaries as we rationalize away the base reality of our existence. These false realities accumulate in our complex cognitive structure. Level of rational development depends on the complexity of our structure; the more complex the structure, the more base reality we have. The more simple the structure, the more that is left to the imaginary.
It becomes a fortress of intellect and reason that barricade avenues of escape as it is developed. Rational fantasy becomes a labyrinth of endless passages of imagination.
Any attempt at rescue is seen as an invading force, intruding to harm. With no one to help you grasp the fleeing objectivity, reality is lost in an illusion of solidarity. The most concise work on this phenomena is in a book by Peter L. Berger, and Thomas Luckmann, called Social Construction of Reality. In the book, he explains the entire structuralization of reality, and fantasy generated by the rational mind. Berger was a major inspiration for me to write my book.

  Social imaginary- *"For John Thompson, the social* **imaginary** *is "the creative and symbolic dimension of the social world, the dimension through which human beings create their ways of living together and their ways of representing their collective life". For Manfred Steger and Paul James "imaginaries are patterned convocations of the social whole. These deep-seated modes of understanding provide largely pre-reflexive parameters within which people imagine their social existence—expressed, for example, in conceptions of 'the global,' 'the national,' 'the moral order of our time.' The imaginary as a Lacanian term refers to an illusion and fascination with an image of the body as coherent unity, deriving from the dual relationship between the ego and the specular or mirror image."* [Andacht, Fernando. *A Semiotic Framework for the Social Imaginary*. Arisbe: The Pierce Gateway, 2000].

Analysis- So by this observation and articulation, a healthy imaginary is a true social collective imaginary, and that the problem is when we are individualized so that it becomes not part of our social existence, but part of our individuated existence. This is where sociopathy progresses to psychopathy. The inner sufferings of the soul are the result of social neurosis that breaks down cognitive development, and leads to them becoming hyper rational, and prone to levels of imaginary that exceed the threshold of what is socially tolerable. Uniformity as a means to create an Illusion of solidarity by means-end rationality to deal with the breakdown of organic solidarity. Concrete solidarity is in the true social existence of hunter/gatherer. This depends on similarity. Organic depends on a system of differentiation and contrary elements working for different purposes, yet supply the needs of those surrounding them. This exists naturally within ecosystems. When we are individualized, we start to become different in all these little ways. This starts to create an organic solidarity. This is fun for a little while, but after individuation reaches a certain point, there is a breakdown in this form of organics, and their many differences extended to the point of great distance between each other in reality, difficult to even share a common reality, resulting in much indifference, and estrangement and ultimately a disintegration of solidarity. The society crumbles as their ability to cooperate with each other breaks down to the point of crisis. When the structured economy collapses, they run for the hills to flee the sudden anarchy.

All this rationalization that democracy can be engineered to make an ideal society where we have all our social needs and moral function for vitality is preposterous. We have been in a state of denial. No matter how bad things get, people keep trying to find different ways to make it work, that only complicates the issues, creating more unforeseen problems. The more freakish it gets, the more we are desensitized to the freakshow. Fromm even warned about robotism in contemporary society. Automatic function mode is a characteristic of a sociopath. Take out the emotional depth of a person, and you have a robot. Once the process is fully onset by the golden age of the democratic society, it continues even to divide all members of family, and household while all are oblivious to this devastation until they are victims to its reality. The destruction of the immediate family structure, also contributes to bringing independence and individualization to the point of absolute.

iii. diagnosis

Sane society- "*normative humanism is based on the assumption that, as in any problem, there are right and wrong satisfactory and unsatisfactory solutions in the problem of human existence. Mental health is achieved if man develops into full maturity according to the characteristics and laws of human nature, mental illness consists in the failure of such development. From this premise the criterion of mental health is not one of individual adjustments to a given social order, but universal for all men*". When it comes down to mental health, it has everything to do with children getting their social needs in an environment conducive to facilitating the establishment of what those needs are intended to bring about in a young soul. Children sit behind a desk all day, which -that in itself- has psychological consequences. It was the upbringing that kept our minds healthy. You had to have all your values set in order by the time you become an adult. We've lost our upbringing. Problem with marriage today can be understood if we imagine two toddlers getting married and having a family. They are not mature enough to even know what they are doing. They more like pretend with their imagination they are grownups. But when it comes to responsibilities and sacrifices necessary, they have no tolerance for each other, and are quickly fighting over their toys. Realistically, a toddler can't be expected to be there for his children anymore than he can fly over the Grand Canyon in a little red wagon. He sees these things in his imagination, but cannot bring them about. Modern man lacks realism because he's living in a fantasy. He's not in the reality of creation being what he really is, a social creature.

There's a difference between diagnosing an individual, and diagnosing a society- "*Important difference between individual and social mental illness, suggests differentiation between two concepts, that of defect and that of neurosis. If a person fails to attain freedom, spontaneity, a genuine expression of self, he may be considered to have a defect. If the majority of members of any given society, we deal with the phenomena of socially patterned defect, all aware of it and not threatened by the experience of being different.*" On page 19, Fromm gives some reference points as to determining societal health, and some determining factors as signs of sickness, "*if he lives under conditions contrary to his nature.*" He references the term "*social neuroses*" from the book "*Civilization and its Discontent*" written by Freud on page 20, to explain a deterioration of man's social needs explaining that a sane society corresponds to the provision of these needs rather than the wants of individuals.

But I consider this feat to achieve this objectivity is only found in the common effort of a collective. Individuals are not coordinated privately, so there is no solution when the problem is in the values of those who don't wish to be coordinated. So the social annihilator continues out of control because everyone wants their own space. Only in the collective commonwealth does the family stay together and avoid the law of contraction, with everyone getting their social needs as they all work and learn together in liberation.

To explain this social neurosis, we need to understand that a patterned defect is something being internalized to a level of frequency among members of society to the point of it becoming an established norm. This can make it so that healthy interaction and socialization is a violation of these "norms' '. This is where substantive rationality becomes so diffuse and contributory to the spreading of the condition in society, because everyone is pressured to conform or be left out. But our conformity leaves us feeling empty inside, because we are starved for real social existence. Key to understanding this plight of man, is in Fromm's writings about the alienated man, and how he's left to society's agenda for him to adapt into a robot he calls an "*automaton*"; *a moving mechanical device made in imitation of a human being.* This is a new form of slavery in repeated mechanical motions in an environment that replaced normal interpersonal interaction with repeated frases and programmed responses. This mundane repetition challenges man to maintain his sanity to the point of desperation. Page 121 refers to the original french term "*alie'ne*". Marx defines it as when man's "*own act to him becomes an alien power standing over and against him, instead of ruled by him.*" [Karl Marx]

Fromm goes on to explain that alienation isn't a modern phenomena, but that we are actually experiencing a modern version of it. There are many forms of alienation depending on the particular society, and at which point human nature is abandoned, and to what particular foreign system they're being conformed to, and the ethical value constellations of the dominating forces within that society. Page 28- key to humanistic psychoanalysis- Freud searched for the basic force which motivates human passions and desires. He believed he found it in *libido*, but Fromm directs it to the "*human situation.*" "*The problem of man's existence, then, is unique in the whole of nature; he has fallen out of nature, as it were*", "*he has lost his home*". [page 25] As structural leaders become more independent, the more their spectrum is confined to the micro, so the macro is ignored for lack of adequate overview. Overseers have to be able to see the big picture, and be macro oriented, or they lack ability. For general populations, levels of sociopathy seem to increase with levels of status.

Example: multitude of voters want to know why micro politician squanders enormous amounts of money on excessive luxury, while we are in a state of economic crisis. But the same goes for those at the bottom of the stratus, who fell through the cracks and needed special help because of unforeseen circumstances, who were devastated and crushed by the apathy they saw when everyone just looked on, leaving them destitute. They didn't even see the apathy until they found themselves in crisis. I'm not all that educated about the terminology of sociology, or social psychology, but I call this phenomena -bottom dwellers viewpoint. Rock bottom is where we find reality, and then mentally escape. There's been a sense of alarm with the levels of heinous crime, and moral degeneration, but nothing to protect conscience and moral standard in our society. Those things are stripped from our society because they hinder mass production and mass consumption. Conscience could not survive general social dysfunctions in the institutions they are assigned to. In high school, It becomes a matter of survival, to not be disposed of socially. The crushed are pushed to the fringe, to go unnoticed.

Dog eat dog begins in the school yard, and only the brutal survive. No love to protect, or to be there for the nurturing of their soul, with meaningful relationships everlasting. For every student that came to school to commit suicide and take others with them, there are thousands who suffer the same things they suffered, even to maybe the same degree, but go unheard and unnoticed. We were all required by law to abandon our children to institutions that do not protect them or provide their social needs, to be chained to their economic *"apparatus"*. The fact that the nation's children would be abandoned to institutions is a devastating blow to the moral force of conscience. When things were getting exceptionally violent on school campuses of big cities of Chicago, New York, Los Angeles, no one ran to the rescue. They were just left there to endure, adapt, and survive.

Now the process of the general population has reached a level of having little if no moral development. Antisocial norms are even in the household. Seven year old child screams and throws a tantrum, and parents respond by pandering to the child and giving them whatever they want. So moral development is programmed in the schema with images of it being normal to scream at someone until you get what you want, even scream at the ones you owe your life to. So now there's even a lack of having the development of the soul essential for receiving communication from the common conscience. So children are denied moral programming. Lying is normal, stealing, disrespecting, cheating, manipulating others for self interests, blatant disrespect and mockery of parents. Soul is not compatible with the spirit. Spirit might not have even been born at this point *"flesh gives birth to flesh, and spirit gives birth to spirit"* [John 3:6] We now live in a sociopathic society, where selfishness is expected, and even praised.

Analysis- The guilt goes unaccounted for, and this is how the conscience is desensitized. Man used to have it in his social life to clear his conscience, to get it off his chest by confessing his sin, and own up to the truth. Man is losing this ability by reasoning away his guilt, and developing a rational intellect to relieve the *"cognitive dissonance"* in the struggle to find consistency in this society, because his networks don't include this vital social function of accountability. But of course any continual unchecked violation of what was the 'original' social norms, will eventually result in losing your sensitivity. All who live in modern society have been infected to various degrees, and it seems to be on the continual progression of insensitivity being internalized into society. Exceptionalism is an antisocial norm that generates strife between men and women, competing instead of contribution to each other- stepping on each other in our dash for cash. School institutions have antisocial norms that are internalized by students that impair their conscience. In strife for social status, others are left out. That part of our conscience to include others as we would want to be included, is desensitized. Now people are exposable, and it's normal. Now there's not much appreciation and concern for consumers, unless they bring the big money. But then it's all about the money. No more taking care of the customers, with customer service standards of care just because you are a customer.

Sociopathy has been the unnamed sickness that so many social psychologists have noted in their documentation, but no one has really gotten down to what the unnamed "sickness" is. The disease Marcuse is talking about is sociopathy. The "lean-to" effect plays into Marcuse's point about the stifling of critical thought, because all subjectivity generally comes from above in the stratus, ending all critical functions of society. Immunity shutdown. The immune system is where moral force can do its part. So the pressure to adapt is quite intense with the alternatives offered under the guise of liberty to *"be enslaved or starve."* [pg 284] in a society that has a shutdown of its immune system. The industrial psychology research findings showed during the boom of the 50's, that money, prestige, and power, were the main incentive for the general population that represented the middle and upper classes.

These are not good building blocks. These incentives perpetuate the increase of opposition to the moral force within, that is continually compromised on greater levels. Selfishness doesn't even know how to build a house so it won't collapse. Too lazy to establish the foundation. Way over confident in abilities because they lack respect and appreciation for those who know how to build. Democracy isn't as it is advertised; a place where there's freedom in the land to live out your ambitions and prosperity. Modern democracy is actually a carefully engineered complex structured system of formal functionalities that aim to guard the establishment, control the population, and generate revenue and leverage over other nation states. It is a wealth and power making machine for the ruling class, and its industries and civilians are cogs that work for their purpose. There are carefully guarded interests and investments that escalate money to the top when the economy is stimulated. This Kirby effect of the apparatus eventually sucks all the money out of the economy until it collapses with 99% subject to the 1% at the top with it all. Exploitation is its beginning, and the means to its end.

Enemy within- we pay more attention to the one with the golden ring, and tell the poor "sit at my feet" (James 2:2). This is how we end up with this parallel between social status, and monetary status I call the "lean to effect." It all comes down to this imbalance of "primary self concern cognition". All levels of stratus appeal to those directly above them, for self interests. This can be seen when a teen is begging mom to let her stay out an extra hour that night, while the toddler is crying to the 8 year old to share the candy, as the 8 year old sneaks into the teens room to get her smart -phone. Each one striving to reach the next strata, to get what they want. Each level is apathetic to the one below. So it all hinges on the dismantling of mechanical solidarity, which results in each family member being self oriented , rather than group oriented. So they compete as individuals because their team orientedness that came from tribal life is gone, allocating the necessity for the whole process.

General population will be disgusted with the apathy of politicians, but have no mercy when someone is holding a sign saying they need help. They will rationalize that the money is wasted on booze or drugs without getting involved in their situation, and then be enraged when someone judges them without even knowing them. That's why it doesn't work. We can't make it so that we can all just think about ourselves, and then expect others to consider our needs and rights as citizens. Apathy is a consequence to this selfish ambition. If we want others to care about us, then we have to care about others. We don't learn to care for others, without taking care of them. This is how the conscience grows strong in moral force and thrives. Care wants to know the need, and so takes the lead to do all that can be done to meet the need. *"Love finds a way."*

b. Paradigm & Perspective

We can see in the emergence of sexual sociopathic behavior in the 30's, how there was a certain level of impairment of sensitivity. The process of sociopathy that resulted in violent rapes actually started in the beginning of the sexual revolution of the roaring 20's. The conscience of both male and female was being desensitized when it came to acts of sexuality, that in the heat of a revolution even gets aggressive. So promiscuity became a norm, and so now there was an established sense of 'it's ok'. 'What's the big deal?' Here the original paradigm of the conscience is that we would be betraying the clan by stealing the highly guarded virginity of the youth of the elders, or committing adultery with their wives. All this kind of behavior would completely destroy an entire clan, or maybe even the whole tribe. That's why the sociopath had to be sent out of the clan, to wander as a vagabond. These are among the greatest acts of betrayal a person could do to another person. That's why it was originally such a shameful thing to do. It's not as immediate, but promiscuity has been destroying our society. Morality is simply being lost in the "real world". It seems simple to see how individualizing people will result in losing all the "why's" of conscience because they are now separated from each other in the private realm. Conscience depends on us being subject to others on a close private interpersonal relation, rather than a distant liberal association. But this act of liberal squandering in itself is an antisocial norm being internalized by social creatures whose conscience is for the very purpose of their vital needs.

Over eating in collective life could bring about years of famine for the whole tribe. The destructive effects of mass consumption are astronomical. These maladies destroy the vitality of societies. Breaking the bond of practical dependence without replacing the practicality with love, turns social creatures into antisocial creatures. As the soul loses its sensory of the spirit, it is replaced by a feeling of emptiness, a void with a deep need to be filled. This is where the connection to the parietal lobe contains the somatosensory cortex, which is essential for processing sensory information from across the body, such as touch, temperature, and pain. This connection in the somatic circuit is to initially be stimulated by meaningful social interaction, as how affectionate love would caress in certain ways; the rubbing of your back when it aiks, or caressing someone's hair. These can all be intertwined with fond memories of intimate moments. The satisfaction only comes when it is sincere love. When our meaningful social interaction is removed, this connection now replaces the stimulation in materialistic pursuits.

The more conscience is diminished, the greater the sense of the void and its demand for stimulation. The core of the soul eventually becomes like a black-hole, at its core an insatiable appetite to consume all. No matter the level of things attained, there lacks real satisfaction of the soul, even if the whole world! were attained, there would remain an even greater level of thirst and hunger to consume, possess and control. Gone completely insane. Consumption hunger is a real sickness that kills mind, body and spirit. Demoralization process is in the achievement of much success for individuals, and blessings of abundance for them. What kills the Affect is when we go beyond our fair share in what God has provided for the whole by his means, and then squander in the face of hunger and suffering. Modernism destroyed his means of provision to cater to the mass consumption. Now man has no rightful place of habitation. All engineered for the purpose of wage slavery. Even the squirrels have this protected right, that man has lost. A sign the sickness is at the helm, is when the structure begins to write vagrancy (go die somewhere) laws for those who don't have money. These go die somewhere laws even prohibit you from asking when you're hungry. Disregarding the vitality in the society we live in, and man's attempt to preserve his own life when caught in a dilemma while everyone mass consumes is nothing but utterly wicked. The next level is when the needy are criminalized for this attempt to survive. This is a mass draconic indoctrination to force suicide on those considered a nuisance. This is where man has gone below the level of an animal. Animals at least take care of their own. We can be redeemed, but it has to be a sincere awakening of the spirit, being brutally honest in facing the wretched condition, and bringing one out of their fantasy and into the stark reality the world is trying to escape with media distraction. We must find the *"fully developed and awakened man"* [sane society page 27].

No freedom of conscience in society- *"The rights and liberties which were such vital factors in the origins and earlier stages of industrial society yield to a higher stage of this society: they are losing their traditional rationale and content."* *"Freedom of thought, speech, and conscience were--just as free enterprise, which they served to promote and protect--essentially critical ideas, designed to replace an obsolescent material and intellectual culture by a more productive and rational one. Once institutionalized, these rights and liberties shared the fate of the society of which they had become an integral part. The achievement cancels the premises."* [Marcuse One Dimensional Man pg, 3-4] If we compromise our conscience to work for sociopaths, then we are essentially adapting to their immoral standards, and their insensitivities. It's just like when a kid is subject to bad influences in the neighborhood, and it changes him as he adapts to the new "norms" within his small network, and follows the examples of the dominating forces, internalizing their set of values.

Liberation depends on conscience- *"All liberation depends on the consciousness of servitude, and the emergence of this consciousness is always hampered by the predominance of needs and satisfactions which, to a great extent, have become the individual's own. The process always replaces one system of preconditioning by another; the optimal goal is the replacement of false needs by true ones, the abandonment of repressive satisfaction."* [Marcuse One Dimensional Man] Economic crisis is from excessive standards of needs, putting an oppressive expectation on citizens to meet the demand. Bureaucratic practical and formal rational action to dominate, with codes of standards incalculable to know the level of impact on civilians, such as vagrancy laws. Homeless are considered criminals for the sake of their displacement.

How else can you explain the endless tickets for violations that suck all the money that could maybe get them out of their situation? Psychological trauma is extensive when involving attempts at survival; sleeping, camping, panhandling? These laws -if we calculate all the 'don'ts' to see what it allows for us to 'do'- they are essentially telling homeless people to go die somewhere. Only sociopaths write 'go die somewhere' laws to make people who need help go away from their places of indulgences in the flesh. It spoils their fun, and makes them feel uncomfortable and messes up their scenery. Those who enforce those laws have to be insensitive to man's plight, his effort to survive, or find his sanity. Poverty as Fromm put it, "*is but a sign of man's enslavement.*" "*Wage slavery will exist as long as a man or an institution that is the master of men.*" So poverty is a sign of man conquering man, but this reality is clouded with a fantasy that says quite the contrary- that the homeless man's fate was just his poor judgment. I've seen so many cases that are far from anything typical. One hard working man simply was a victim of his wife dying, and after proving his innocence in court, he got out of jail with nothing to his name but the clothes on his back. House, truck and job- gone. But the general story involves serious levels of child abuse.

Driving the needle deeper- Research also determined that the old deficit oriented approach by structure's criminalization actually drives the needle deeper. Drug rehabs have a phenomena of those who were once there, condescending on those there now. The old term for this was 'forgetting where you came from.' In their fantasy, they're above all that. But in reality they aren't. I have experienced this institutional cruelty on an interactive participant level.

It would trigger me and I would become indignant. Still do. This has not only proven to be ineffective, but actually harmful, causing the victims of child abuse to relive these traumatic events. The trigger is in the apathetic authority, that is harsh and insensitive to their needs. Police officers have been among our most noble examples of servitude and bravery, even sacrificing themselves for the safety of others. But there's also the opportunity of sheer tyranny reigning unfettered. These are the inevitable number who are sick, and have made their way into places of authority. They too might be traumatized, or just lacking moral value in a state of adolescence.

The flesh is oppressive- *"Most of the prevailing needs to relax, to have fun, to behave and consume in accordance with the advertisements, to love and hate what others love and hate, belong to this category of false needs. Such needs have a societal content and function which are determined by external powers over which the individual has no control; the development and satisfaction of these needs is heteronomous. No matter how much such needs may have become the individual's own, reproduced and fortified by the conditions of his existence; no matter how much he identifies himself with them and finds himself in their satisfaction, they continue to be what they were from the beginning-products of a sodety whose dominant interest demands repression. The prevalence of repressive needs is an accomplished fact, accepted in ignorance and defeat, but a fact that must be undone in the interest of the happy individual as well as all those whose misery is the price of his satisfaction."* [Marcuse 1975] Tie in- so Marcuse' point is essentially that our materialistic values that we replaced with spiritual values of family, and brotherhood, become our own tyrannical oppressor.

antithesis- Negative aspects of the patriarchal complex are hierarchy, oppression, inequality, submission. These aspects are not always part of the patriarchy. Many, even most aren't socially stratified, they are just family members. Even the patriarch leader is just a father figure. The conflict in patriarchy seemed to come by masses, and strivings outside of nomadic life. Clans have to remain relatively small, and content with love.

i. functionalism

moral force- Sane Society, Page 47, Fromm goes into the close connection between the fatherly and motherly figures and moral principles. Freud's *superego* relates conscience as only from the father's commands and prohibitions. But Fromm goes deeper into how the mother builds on this with reminders of duty, love, and forgiveness of others as well as yourself. But it all begins with the father. Process of maturity brings us to being our own father, mother, and child. Father is faithful to tell us what we "*ought*" to do. He rewards obedience, and punishes disobedience. The connection to the collective is that fatherhood was originally a patriarchy. Remove the patriarchy, you remove the fatherhood, and the motherhood, and remove the moral force that becomes a process of demoralization. The result is a generation of sociopaths by the third and fourth generation. There are scriptures in the Bible that warn of spiritual death and indicate that the duration of the process of demoralization to be by the "*third and fourth generation.*" [Exo 20:5, 34:7, Num 4:18, Duet, 5:9] The demoralization of the Amorites: "*In the fourth generation your descendants will come back here, for the sin of the Amorites has not yet reached its full measure.*" [Gen 15:16]. Also "*I, the Lord your God, am a jealous God, punishing the children for the sin of the parents to the third and fourth generation of those who hate me.*"

- Durkheim stated that the family is a social institution subject to a cultural evolution, with the conjugal family as its final conclusion. It is not merely a biological affair, but has moral and judicial implications which are protected by the collective in which the family is embedded.

The original paradigm was the origins of our mentality; our mind and spirit in the initial intention of life. The moral force is encoded in us by our own needs we receive from those who nurture. We know we need food, water, air, somewhere to sleep, warmth when its cold, empathy when we get hurt, medicine when we're sick, understanding when we make big mistakes, help in understanding the world, and how we fit into it. We know that others need these things just as much. But if these things aren't being established in our life, we lack moral development. Others can replace the mother and father's role and establish this moral force of spirit through representations and confrontations, the commands and prohibitions of the Father's word, and the reminders of duty, love, and forgiveness from the mother. Others can play this role if trust and transparency is achieved in their relationship. Our conscience originally functioned within the collective as a governing sensitivity to remain together as a family.

The function of spirit had to do with the close affection in our interdependency. The role changes when one is liberated from this interdependency, and now this force has to tug and pull, and try to find cooperation. Even this effect would demonstrate the vital cut-off that occurs from independence, and the loss of harmony of function as a social being. The whole purpose of having a sensitive conscience is in developing and maintaining relationships with others. It comes from the primal element in our being. We can see upon observation the purpose of being sensitive to others, and how it is essential for collective life of togetherness that brings a wholesome vitality and sense of security.

Affective Sensitivities- contriteness, remorse, forgiveness, understanding. Contriteness is feeling sorry for what you've done, and a wanting to make it right. This is counterbalanced with the sensitivity to be merciful and have forgiveness and understanding. Purpose only transpires in meaningful social life and sustainability, this is where moral value is found. Conscientiousness is care and genuine concern for the wellbeing of others so as to be aware of their needs beforehand. Truthfulness is a sensitivity to tell the truth and admit to it if we go off, this comes about by genuine relationship with those we directly descended from, or later in life by family of choice, and can only be developed by subjectivity to others in private matters.

Interpersonal Sensitivities- authenticity, humility, honesty, trustworthiness. Authenticity is lost by lack of spiritual function *"Actions have to be in congruence with beliefs and desires in order for a person to be authentic"* [Kierkegaard]. Mirror effect occurs, blending in for ulterior operation. Delusions of grandeur correlate with collective fantasy. Independence severs connection to see the great worth in others. Only left to see worth in self, or have an adverse response of worthlessness. The worth and gifts that one has to offer is discovered in the exchanging of vital dependency. True social involvement is where we find our proper worth, and the worth of others. These attributes of the conscience are established by relation and true social interaction- having appreciation of others by dependence on them, relying on each other in meaningful ways. They are first processed cognitively as in what we do. The reasons for these behaviors are later learned in application, more likely normally would be during adolescence. But it is in the togetherness that these things persevere in a person, so that when they've borne fruit, the father's work was well done after much investment. Modern society has robbed us all of our family life, where we just grind away at the money machine. The four interpersonal sensitivities come from a pure motive, and sincere faith of proper value.

Lifestyle Sensitivities- Veriant antonyms are: contentment, productive, contributing, purposeful. Being a part of a bigger purpose rather than just stimulating your senses. We lose purpose in creating our own little world. Somehow meaningful purpose involves meaningful experiences with other people. These are experiences you have in true social societies, not antisocial societies. Hell is the ultimate destination of individualism.

Social Sensitivities- cooperative, supportive, moral, yielding. The most relied upon source of spiritual guidance and understanding comes from the scriptures in the Bible. The original, unadulterated pure gospel, was restoring a people to the original paradigm. Acts 2 and 4 explains how all the believers left their own lives under the autonomy of the Roman democracy, and annulled their contract with Ceasar and returned to patriarchy. John 17:21-23 Yahshua prays for all who receive his apostles: *"that all of them may be one, Father, just as you are in me and I am in you. May they also be in us so that the world may believe that you have sent me. I have given them the glory that you gave me, that they may be one as we are one I in them and you in me—so that they may be brought to <u>perfect unity</u>. Then the world will know that you sent me and have loved them even as you have loved me."*

God, being his mighty Word, comes with urgent warnings of death, and the necessary sacrifice of our own pursuits to find restoration. God is spirit, so there is spiritual life, and spiritual death. Spiritual life can be seen in expressions of care, remorse for those who suffer, mercy for those lost and in need, servitude with a humble heart, repentance, sincerity. This is all from our spirit that brings a moral presence to the atmosphere. The gospel came as a remedy to sociopathy; a spiritual sickness that causes social dysfunction and moral deterioration. This begins by establishing a patriarchy unique in the sense of it being a family by choice. *"Whoever does not gather with me, scatters."* (Luke 11:23) The word *"gathering"* gives the strong sense of bringing together a family. God's family. In understanding the fatherhood of the patriarchy, you see how people living individually independent of each other is like they are all scattered. I've seen it because I lived both; individual independence, and in a collective interdependence under a commonwealth.

Here the true collective mind of God calls his people back into the true collective mind. But Acts 2 & 4 wasn't a legitimate prescribed order, it was an act of freedom and has to remain that way. I've experienced that it can become law, and then it's back to practicality and meaningless legalism in everything from food, to clothing, to just about everything that would make a person an individual. This is a torturous process that isn't so loving. It's not a ministry of compassion, but judgment and condemnation of sin. But just as the Apostle Paul wrote in Romans 7:7, the law is still righteous and good. Spirit seeks out true community, and to leave self life and social bounding to establish social life, but generally can't find it within reach. Spirit longs for meaningful communion, while the individual goes on ignoring this need and seeks various means of *stimuli*, not realizing the need is for his eternal destiny to be vitally connected and flourishing in the spiritual realm by the time his third dimensional existence terminates.

The constant stimulation of the senses is a coping mechanism to ease the feeling of emptiness for lack of fulfillment that brings true satisfaction in the soul. Mass consumption is a sign of an acute level of the condition. Conscious efforts to wean must coincide with complete social restoration and fulfillment of purpose for life.

Highest in moral authority- *"The confrontation of shared representations within a society gives these collective representations a greater vitality, which largely surpasses the vitality of individual representations. This way of conceptualizing consciousness has several consequences. First, Durkheim concludes a split within the human mind between an individual and a collective consciousness where the latter appears as "an echo resounding within ourselves of a force that is alien, one moreover superior to that which we are ourselves" "Second, because of its greater vitality the collective consciousness appears as a moral force. It is also the strongest form of authority. When a certain representation or act goes against these collective representations, against the moral order and greatest authority, this provokes a heavy emotional response from the group."(Durkheim, 1984 [1893], p. 56).*

Restoration- is a spiritual process of making atonement with the Father Spirit, who restores our spirit by the teachings he gave his son Yahshua that is food and medicine for our spirit. To grow in him is to have his word grow in our heart as we remain in step with his word. The moral force of the spirit knows of the supreme force of the father spirit, who calls our spirit to the upper calling, to establish the vitality of the supreme force of love on earth as it is in heaven. Our spirit wants to respond to this, but is at odds with the will of the individual and isn't congruent. We have to find harmony with this moral force, and not wrestle with the authority within, but surrender and yield to its persuasions and expectations. Another thing encoded in the conscience is a sense of one's fair share. This is lost when given the opportunity to have way more than you need, without accountability to others who don't have enough. There's even law enforcement to guard against this accountability. When it comes to collectives, has been common among their leaders, who by their power and influence, take more than their fair share and fatten themselves. Result is apathy which its level depends on excessiveness. But the moral force alone is left with no purpose without being confirmed in the subjectivity of close, private, interpersonal relationships.

Doctrine of conscience- the most concise explanation of the conscience, and how it functions: Romans 2:15 *"They show that the requirements of the law are written on their hearts, their consciences also bearing witness, and their thoughts sometimes accusing them and at other times even defending them."* This was a point Paul was making for those who haven't heard the law or the gospel, but have a natural law encoded in their conscience that governs behavior. Here's some explanations of maintaining a healthy conscience: Acts 24:16 *"So I strive always to keep my conscience clear before God and man."* Job 27:6 *"I will maintain my innocence and never let go of it; my conscience will not reproach me as long as I live."* These are examples of maintaining a healthy conscience by "innocence". Innocence isn't just not doing wrong things, or making mistakes. There is the element of clearing the conscience of guilt by admission, confession, and repentance. Examples: 2 Sam 24:10 *"David was conscience-stricken after he had counted the fighting men, and he said to the Lord, "I have sinned greatly in what I have done. Now, Lord, I beg you, take away the guilt of your servant. I have done a very foolish thing."* These scriptures are the instruction manual for the spirit; how to feed and nurture, and to engage in healthy spiritual life to preserve and strengthen.

Documentation of restoring conscience: 2 Cor 7:8-13 *Even if I caused you sorrow by my letter, I do not regret it. Though I did regret it—I see that my letter hurt you, but only for a little while— yet now I am happy, not because you were made sorry, but because your sorrow led you to repentance. For you became sorrowful as God intended and so were not harmed in any way by us. Godly sorrow brings repentance that leads to salvation and leaves no regret, but worldly sorrow brings death. See what this godly sorrow has produced in you: what earnestness, what eagerness to clear yourselves, what indignation, what alarm, what longing, what concern, what readiness to see justice done. At every point you have proved yourselves to be innocent in this matter.* This scripture is a prime example of being brought out of a fantasy, and into the reality of guilt, and the spirit is awakened and the soul entering into the restoration process through the forgiveness that came after the sorrowful plea of a contrite heart. Reality is, man was created and commanded to be a good steward of God's creation, including the highest form of his creation, that of his own kind.

Page 230, Fromm goes into what we all got to do, but I think the reality is, that all are called, but only a few chosen, to surrender to the striving for the helm, to receive their portion written in their conscience, and let the swindler swindle, and the betrayer betray. For it is written *"vengeance belongs to me"* says the Lord God *"I will repay"*. We have to leave room for God's judgment. The few will enter by their surrender of the frenzy, and to be rogue of those perishing. Let their noble patriotism be seen for what it is, and should be for all. To be the alternative for the rest of the few who will awaken to the call to return to the cause of the spirit.

Out of necessity, man's time had to be occupied with doing his vital part, his mind had to be fixed on the needs of the clan, because they all depended on him, as they took care of his needs as he depended on them. He knew that if no one did their part, the clan would suffer and parish. Lives depended on him. There wasn't so much of a problem with an imbalance of self concern cognition. They were one. But this was not the entire plan for man, he had to go through a process so that by liberation from the practicality of the collective, he would have a dependency based on love, a supreme vitality. Love would be the force behind his actions out of the abundance of the heart. God also desires unique personalities and characteristics that make a person special as is the argument for individuation. But this has to be coordinated into the purpose of love, or it becomes narcissistic.

So once individualized, one returns by the call to the collective, but out of love, not practicality which has proven to be insufficient motivation for returning to, and maintaining the group. It's when this process of individuation just continues without the return by the call, that results in creating hell on earth. Dependence has to not be practical, but out of an expression of the heart. This can only be done in liberation. We must first possess our life, before we can offer it. So liberation is essential for matters of the heart. Love is by choice, and it can't come about by force.

Liberty page 318 (sane society), "*A man is only free under three conditions:*

- 1. Economic freedom- money by money makes possible the exploitation of man by man
- 2. Intellectual freedom- we can choose, if we know enough to make the comparison.
- 3. Moral freedom- passion enslaves, needs coherent life activity consistent with expectations of others

Paul explained it was for the purpose of "equality." In 2 Cor 8:13-15, Paul is urging the Corinthians to give up their abundance to share with the Macedonian church who were in extreme poverty. Even though the issue was between communities, it was the same as with individuals. Starting from verse 13; "*Our desire is not that others might be relieved while you are hard pressed, but that there might be equality. At the present time your plenty will supply what they need, so that in turn their plenty will supply what you need. Then there will be equality, as it is written: "He who gathered much did not have too much, and he who gathered little did not have too little (he quotes Exodus 16:18).*"" Here he uses the example of the bread that fell from heaven, as an analogy to explain how it was portioned out equally in the community, to show God's equal love and concern for all of them, not wanting any of them having more than they need, while others don't have enough.

Moses said that the Lord commanded that the people were to go out at sunrise, and gather all the bread and bring it in, and then to take an omer for each person in your tent. And when the Israelites did as they were told, it says; "*some gathered much, some little. And when they measured it by the omer, he who gathered much, did not have too much, and he who gathered little did not have too little.*" I would like to pose some questions; should those who gathered more than they needed get to keep it? What do all you model Americans think? What would justice do with the scale? Should it be "finders keepers losers weepers"? Is it not a crime to squander in the face of need? These are basic moral concepts of the conscience. How can we support equality and the right to unlimited acquisition at the same time? It's not even the fairness ethic anymore.

The same goes for work. There was a problem with some people in the communities not doing their fair share of work, but were becoming idle. So Paul had given them this instruction: "If a man will not work, he shall not eat. We hear that some among you are idle. They are not busy; they are busybodies. Such people we command and urge in the Lord Jesus Christ to settle down and earn the bread they eat (2 Tim 3:10-12)." That didn't mean to not offer alms to the hungry in the streets judging them that they just are lazy and don't want to work. You have to know the story behind each one as to how they ended up in that situation. It was in reference to people living in a community and having a common pot that everyone lived out of. God doesn't want it where people are not sharing in the work load either, but everyone to be yoked together. But there also was an instance where Paul was talking about orphans, who had to learn to stop stealing, and earn their keep, bear their load, and the load of others.

That good news was mainly for the poor and oppressed. The rich were welcome, but they had to give up all that wealth to join in the family of poor folk who take care of each other, a place where the poor are held in high regard as it's written in James 1:9- "*Believers in humble circumstances ought to take pride in their high position. But the rich should take pride in their humiliation - since they will pass away like a wild flower. For the sun rises with scorching heat and withers the plant; its blossom falls and its beauty is destroyed. In the same way, the rich will pass away even while they go about their business.*" James wrote that because things were going back to the ways of the world where people have more than others, and they were paying special attention to the man with the gold ring, and telling the poor to sit at their feet. A perfect example to explain the "lean to affect." So he was bringing them back to their senses, and humbling them saying *"you humiliate the poor" "has not God chosen the poor to be rich in faith and to inherit his kingdom?"*. In the days of Job, those who exploited the economy were told that they must redistribute the money to the poor, *"His children must make amends to the poor; his own hands must give back his wealth."* Job 20:10 This was to make amends with God. *Job 24:4-5 "They thrust the needy from the path and force all the poor of the land into hiding. Like wild donkeys in the desert, the poor go about their labor of foraging food; the wasteland provides food for their children.*

ii. conflict-

Documentation of desensitizing the conscience in liberation pathway- here's an example of Paul explaining to the church how the gentiles had lost "all sensitivity", and gave themselves over to sensuality- an indication of the conscience being desensitized in the process of relieving and immediate emotional demand in the pathway by liberation. Eph 4:19 *"So I tell you this, and insist on it in the Lord, that you must no longer live as the Gentiles do, in the futility of their thinking. They are darkened in their understanding and separated from the life of God because of the ignorance that is in them due to the hardening of their hearts. Having lost all sensitivity, they have given themselves over to sensuality so as to indulge in every kind of impurity, and they are full of greed."* Paul was talking about these Gentile ways, which were Greek ways -there traditional ways within their democracy provided by Caesar. *"You, my brothers and sisters were called to be free. But do not use your freedom to indulge the flesh; rather, serve one another humbly in love."* [Gal 5:13]. This verse is a documentation that explains not using freedom for indulging in the flesh, and then uses an example of depending on each other *"serve one another humbly in love."*, a written prescription of taking care of others as the remedy for a healthy conscience which would stand opposed to the inclination of self sufficiency. These are the two concepts in the battle between good and evil.

Documentation of exposure pathway- Here's an example of how the conscience can be wounded by the acts of others: 1 Cor 8:12 *"When you sin against them in this way and wound their weak conscience, you sin against Christ."* It mentions that the conscience can be "wounded", and also "weak". Wounded in the sense of something living, that can be hurt. I question the potential level of the wound and the possibility of the spirit receiving a fatal wound. Weak suggests that it has lost sensitivity. Confirmation by the documentation of a certain level of sociopathy. James 1:10-11 *"But the rich should take pride in their humiliation—since they will pass away like a wild flower. For the sun rises with scorching heat and withers the plant; its blossom falls and its beauty is destroyed. In the same way, the rich will pass away even while they go about their business*." What part of him is dying as he goes about his business?? Could it be his conscience that he's betraying? As an example of affectual rationality, the parable in Luke 16 of the rich man and Lazarus, how is it that Lazerous died out in the elements of exposure and starvation, and it had nothing to do with the hoarding of resources and mass consumption?   The rational structured system will tell you it was all the poor man's fault for making bad choices in his life, (without so much as knowing the situation). But it's written that "even the dogs licked his wounds", meaning, 'even the dogs had more mercy on him than the rich man.' To a humanist, that is like saying the dogs were more human than the rich man. Or, more humane.

Maddening wine- People are going out of their mind in the political arena because they keep doing the same thing and expecting a different result. By definition, the political arena is a place of complete insanity. It is the epicenter of the sickness. What needs to be understood is that corrupt politicians who can hardly agree on anything, and squander enormous amounts of money in times of crisis is the fruit of individualism. They were taught to live it up!, get as much as you can for your-self. The ones who are going to succeed in election, are the real go-getters, in a monetary way of speaking. That is what the whole system was based on. So if we endorse this form of society, then it is the fruit of our works. It's not them. It's us. Our selfishness is the problem; everyone's selfishness. There's all this finger pointing and blame game going on and people are missing the point of what the problem is. The issue isn't all the things they're yelling about in congress. The real problem is a social issue. It's related to the problem in the homes where marriages are falling apart very quickly and children are left with no consistency in development. Children aren't being parented, they're being institutionalized. Why the big question about mental illness? It seems very obvious. The structure and big corps pushed out the humanist observations made by qualified social psychologists that warned of very serious dangers to family and mental health, and those warnings were disregarded. Overruled. There wasn't a chance against the powers that be.

So whenever these deficits are brought to the table, the money goes to universities that employ professors to look at brain imaging equipment and scratch their heads. All of this is to make people think we're doing something about it when we really are avoiding the real situation that has happened since the beginning of our golden age -that our society has been completely demoralized to the point of utter corruption. The sign of this is vagrancy laws, and actual enforcement of dehumanization to the point of committing crimes against humanity. But in their fantasy, crimes against humanity and terrorism only happen overseas in Iran, and Pakistan, and Afghanistan. It's a version of the *"my shit don't stink"* syndrome. Another sign of immaturity. Consistent with the vain ego characteristic of primary type. Ask any of the teachers, and they'll tell you *"it's not my job to parent your child"*. Even if you give them all your time at the end of the day, the things that would undo your parenting have already been going on all day at school. There has to be consistency, or there's no point. So this is a sure fire way to end up with toddlers having badges, and guns, and gavels, C-130 Air Ships, bajillion dollar industries. The grim reality is that individualism cuts off man's social life, so that he has none. But man is a social creature, so his created purpose is taken away, and he's left alone in the little box of his own world, where he becomes more and more estranged and indifferent from others. But the problem continues because there are very few who want to see what part of the problem is in them, and facing that. If we all did that, then we might actually start doing something. But that would be defeating the opportunity to live for your-self. So where do we draw the line? The conflict seems to be in the dichotomy of trying to have your cake and eat it too. People want to live for themselves, and find true love, and have a big loving family that functions well and all love each other, but you can't have both. Selfishness gives birth to selfishness. Love gives birth to love. They are contrary to one another. If you gain one, you forfeit the other. If you love one, you despise the other. Love denies self to take care of the needs of others, the most pressing and dire needs first. Love is unmerited. Love can't be bought and paid for, but takes giving up everything to have it. If we choose individual independence, then we don't agree to worship God who is love on his terms, we forfeit love. If we choose Greek philosophers, we are not believers. It's not that I think they should have never been, they are all still a part of God's plan on earth for those who believe, and for those who choose not to believe. How can I give up my life for God, if it wasn't first given to me by the efforts of man? But God's purpose was ultimately to create heaven on earth, where there isn't politics and the corruption of man's selfish desires. So those things will pass away.

Thesis- liberation causes us to become individuated, differentiated, and in various forms of colors and ideas. As we become more different, we become more indifferent. Theoretically we increase in denominations that have different perspectives on certain gnostics. This is a process of dividing us all from each other, rather than uniting as it is written *"that they may be one, as you and I are one Father "* (Jn 17:21-23). He prayed that the night before he was crucified, and it had everything to do with his life's work. The paradigm that would unite us is the collective interdependence of hunter gatherers by choice and not forced adaptation. The individual paradigm divides, and conquers all for the few. Whereas, the hunter gatherer paradigm brings in their kill for the many. Which one would be the moral force of conscience? Individual mind has gathered all this fascinating data about the vast universes of knowledge and the information of physics and astronomy, and the spectacle of technology, but socially we are completely retarded, and hardly able to grasp the rudiments. True socialization was based on a collective paradigm. Marxism resulted in communism, but even that isn't the collective paradigm. It's forced reversal of the process of individuation and so it ends up in slavery and torture. The collective clans weren't being forced to be a collective. They were a true collective because that's all they knew, and they were content with that. Once Greek and Roman democracy exploded on the scene, they were mesmerized by the wonders of the empire, and so collective life was abandoned, not realizing the consequences; that eventually everything that was good, family and fellow man, would be destroyed. Now we think family is just a bunch of biological organisms from the same gene pool, and home is a box with windows.

Man is still oblivious to the consequences because of the slow rate of progression, over generations and generations. We don't realize what was lost, because we haven't had it so much in our day. By the multitude of information we have looked at to support my hypothesis, I feel safe coming to the conclusion that these matters are spiritual, and that psychophysiology has no remedy, or even orientation as to the nature of the problem leaving no point of reference for either diagnosis or hope of prognosis. Most of what needs to be determined empirically has already been covered by Emile Durkheim in his determinations of origins of conscience coming from the collective, and that the will of the individual creates a dual with the moral force within. Research must contest the notion that there is no succession to this dual of conscience and the individual. Max Weber also covered a lot of the groundwork in his discovering the development of the rational mind at the point of liberation. Now 100 years later we've seen over the decades the stages of the process. From trivial entertainment, to rebellion, to indulgence, to heinous acts of torture, mutilation, and overt satanic worship. The point of this research is to come to the conclusion as to the cause of sociopathy, but what has hindered anything substantial in this research is the effect of the sickness, which is a rational fantasy generated by the rational mind assigning unsubstantiated definitions to actions and words. It is at this point that the research conducted must reveal this breakdown, to show the true reality of what is happening. The conflict of action versus perception must be seen and established, and the pathogen detected by observation. For the removal of definition in words and action is a removal of consciousness- the awareness by which moral force can deliberate, or even be established for that matter.

c. Method: Scientific

    i. Variable Sampling

        hypothesis

    ii. Empirical Evidence

        participant observation

        data

    iii. Correlations to hypothesis

        spurious correlation

    iv. Primal Data- The American Nightmare

        conclusion

    v. Interpretative framework

    vi. literature review

    i. Variable Sampling

Probability Sample: night security- Sandbox is my homeless friend who works hard to gather rocks and plantlife, to create beautiful miniature landscapes and make the world "beautiful again". He praises God for His wonders. He's a very sensitive man, who's very generous with the little he has. He, and I, and several others are a network of caretakers. We've all been there for each other in times when we were hungry. We've all depended on each other to survive, while also helping others outside our network. But It hurts Sand Box when they just take without giving back. He often cries because of what is happening to the world, and doesn't understand why people don't love each other, or even care. When he sees acts of kindness, he gets a big smile on his face, and is overjoyed. But he does have his grumpy moments. He worked very hard creating a rock garden, full of beautiful plants and flowers and little trees. He introduced a three dimensional art to me, that I soon developed a desire for. But his beautiful rock garden across oceanside blvd was all dug up and destroyed. One night we were sharing a spot under the overhang at the old Chase Bank building that was empty. It was in the middle of winter with freezing cold temperatures, and raining. If you get wet in the winter, you are in danger of hypothermia. While we lay there trying to sleep, a security guard shows up in a car and says, "You can't sleep there". We said, "but it's raining and we need to stay dry. He said "not my problem". I quoted proverbs 14:31 "anyone who oppresses the poor, is in contempt of their maker." He said, "Just doin my job."

Representative Sample: Soup kitchen- pastor of soup kitchen turns away most of the hungry because of drug and alcohol testing requirements. I myself tested positive for opiates, which would indicate probable heroin use, but I don't use opiates. Members of the soup kitchen ministry talk to me like I'm a liar, and send me on my way without food. Us homeless are indignant and see the apathy. Several weeks later I'm invited for just a day to hear a sermon and have a hot dog. I talked to the pastor about the botched drug test, and he said "yeah there's this thing about poppy seeds". I responded with "but Jesus commanded us to feed the hungry, even love our enemy". Pastor says "yeah, well we still have to obey Caesar." "Obey Caesar?" I asked. "Yeah, you know, he said give unto Caesar what is Caesar's." I guess he interprets this to mean that we're supposed to obey Caesar. I said "he was talking about paying taxes. He wasn't saying, 'only obey God and feed the hungry if Caesar lets you.' I observed a hint of contention in the air, that makes me think he might be experiencing cognitive dissonance. I respond with "I don't know about this 'obey Caesar' excuse to not obey the commands of God." Pastor says, "we're all still one in Christ brother, just come and have a hot dog and hear a sermon." Suddenly he's got to go, so he jumps into his new truck, and drives away. I wasn't so much feelin the one-ness. The thing he said about the poppy seeds did make me think of all those kaiser rolls at the yellow deli though.

Variable Hypothesis-

Apathy- dependent variable: somehow the security guard's job includes sentencing me and Sandbox to death, although I was glad we survived it. But the threat to our lives was very real, and was an undocumented empowerment to hinder our attempts at survival, and even put our lives in danger to just do what the money says we're supposed to do. But in his imagination, he is doing what is the most important thing to do, have a job and make money. He thinks it's all understandable -that we have to go and face possible hypothermia and death- and that his hands are totally washed from it because he is just doing his job. He is completely unaware that he has no value or regard for the preservation of human life. That is what society has put into this merciless man; that homeless people should have to suffer horribly and die, and he's fine with this as a norm in society. 'Not his problem'. He wasn't the least bit concerned that we could die. The pastor spoke to me as if we were one in Christ, after giving me the apathetic cold shoulder with 'sorry, have to obey Caesar, so we can't feed you when you're hungry'. He even says it with a big smile, which I have to say was very painful. Very strange phenomena. Totally free to have more than he needs, and not be subject to his brother who goes hungry and lives outside. If I try to hold him accountable the way a tribesman would be accountable to his fellow kin, he would just call Caesar's centurion guards to take me away. And somehow this is all what Jesus wants?

Rational pathogen- independent variable: rational pathogens for social action to draw conclusions that create perception. These rationalities are placing definitions on certain actions to equate them as violations of ethical code of conduct. The pastor was displaying a typical traditional rational pathogen; "we're still one in Christ brother". This shows a disconnect from the definition of what makes us one. And an inclination to make you think they are on your side while they are apathetic. This develops over a long time of rationalizing to relieve the tensions of homeostasis in an alien environment consisting of a denial form of traditional rationale, that we're still one in Christ when most everyone is divided and only really loving themselves. Placing the wrong definitions on actionis obscures the fact of inner motivations, and is part of substantive rationality that influences their sense of reality to tolerate actions. This is to relieve them from moral misery. There are also value rationalities to relieve the immediate emotional demands by designating things as needs when they aren't. The pastor is displaying the typical *Calvin Work Ethic* take on predestination, that coincides with ancient practical theoretical rationality. They think we don't have money cuz we don't got it right with Jesus. Maybe they don't understand that's why Jesus told the rich to sell everything and give to the poor, so he could bless them. But they tell us, 'if you get it right with Jesus, he's gonna bless you too.' And then send us back to our bush. This comes from a postulate rational pathogen that they have more because they are special to God. This helps them squander in the face of poverty without having to feel guilty. But what it communicates to us is that we need money to make God happy and want us. Homeless need to be psychologically protected even from churches that say we're evil and don't deserve to live because we're homeless and don't have money. The ethic has been habitualized into society, so he probably doesn't even know where it comes from. But still, rationalization is the same.

Awakenings- intervening variable: Includes documentation of sudden positive responses in emotional dilemmas demonstrating the initial awakening and functioning of conscious spirit. Deep emotional responses are a sign of restoration. This would result in a positive change in behavior regularities, and a readjustment of value clusters once pathogen was detected, and the reality brought the real words to the actions that are now repented of. It is this vital breakdown of accountability to those depended upon in closer interpersonal relations that disengage moral force in decision making, and is the point where the liberation pathway lays the grounds and opens the gates for exposure. Once there is no Affect, there is no level of reasoning that can be made other than stark direct control. They've lost that ability. But for those of us still sensitive, it is up to ourselves to open this door of accountability, or the process is only momentary for lack of consistency in subjectivity. <u>True social existence must be restored for consistency to support corrective emotional responses, and nurture them to grow and function now emotionally with a new mind and heart.</u>

Learning service site:

streets of oceanside ca   2019 - 2021

ii. Empirical Evidence

participant observation-

Ethnography: small semi-nomadic society among the homeless. The setting is the streets of Oceanside California; a four block radius where several of us live in the camps at the far corner of a field, or in the bushes, under a bridge, small niches and crevices between businesses, or right out in public areas. There are a few common areas we have. At the east end there are the drunks, who stay right around the Taco Bell, liquor store, and the Am/Pm. On the west side, there are several tweekers and heroin addicts that hang around a McDonalds. Unlike the drunks, they have a complex network of hustlers, drug dealers, hookers, and slingers. Maverick has been homeless there for over 30 years. His biggest customers are the business owners who come to him for drugs. He's the informer of the situation on the streets, when something "goes down." Maverick says business owners are a big part of crime that goes on in the streets, but it's the homeless who take the blame.

Interactions- streets have different levels of dependence and independence. There are certain levels of sharing and stealing with the general population, though they call this stealing "taxing". There's usually some reason for the taxation, some wrong done that wasn't accounted for, etc. Some of us are caretakers, who share what we have to take care of each other and demonstrate an indication of the presence of conscience. Some are particularly independent, they will barter for goods, but steel and hustle when they need to rely on others. There is some level of exchange between the two groups, but generally they are separate. Exposure pathway is more in the realm of affectual rationality- usually in moments of reverting to L1 (survival mode), or L2 emotional outburst or opportunity. It is a non-deliberate, in the moment, process of desensitizing. In these cases that I've seen in the past with the homeless, much of their rationality is in the realm of what they call "taxing". This is where debts are withheld, and possessions confiscated as punishment for violations.

Behaviors- there is a common toughness, though different variations and degrees depending on levels of exposure. Apathy is common among the far majority, but some to the level of antisocial behavior. The struggle to survive is resisted by authorities, and store owners, so all experience explosions of discontent and anger because of the circumstances created in this environment. There's a general sense of being overwhelmed by the impossible expectations society has on them, and levels of desperation test a person's moral threshold. Police busted your camp, and cut your tent that protected you from the rain, and in being displaced, you are in sudden survival mode. You were pushed out into the rain during the night, and you and all your belongings are completely soaked. Mold is a threat to you losing your belongings, and you've been freezing all night, and have to find a way to get things dry, and store owners say "get your shit out of here", and you explode because of the apathy you see when you are trying to survive. After your epic journey to settle in somewhere, the process starts all over again. You never know what's coming next. Limbic system unable to stabilize. They need to see you aren't looking down on them and just gonna shine them on before they come to reach tenant three; trust and transparency.   They only really know when you've turned the other cheek after they have said some hurtful shit, or stole something, or lied to you, or just never paid you back. Turning the other cheek is not turning your heart away from them, and cutting them off after they react.   Those from small towns, still seem to be sensitive in their conscience, and willing to share with those in need. A certain down to earthness about them, and generally display shock and discontent with the apathy in society. Those of us who've been lifers on the street, know that often it is also the Mexicans that don't even speak english that are the most sensitive and generous. They would come up and lay a blanket on top of you. This correlates to Durkheim's observation of the collective conscience. They are usually also of the older generations. The younger generations are generally apathetic, and materialistic, and very low on conscientiousness. Because of this moral schism, they are in conflict with each other.

The typical cycle that perpetuates their plight is that these abandoned ones try to go to places where they can get food and supplies, and then are triggered when the suppliers are critical of them, and come over them with their authority while apathetic to their vulnerability and desperate situation. This hits a very painful wound you received when being devastated by the brutal reality that they were discarded by family and friends, then, "fuck you, I'm not a piece of shit!!!". The outburst causes public estrangement, and people are looking at you like you are some kind of psycho, and call the police because they have to deal with "the problem." This drives a worthlessness into them and internal oppression to deal with something they are not equipped to deal with alone. They are pushed away from where they can get vitals, because of their dependencies, but are trapped in a very unstable situation. Even a doctor would be saying that they need medical assistance to deal with those dependencies, that people die from in the attempt to deal with it themselves.   They are in desperate need emotionally, and psychologically because of the level of suffering, and the need to ease the suffering is their hook to these dependencies they fall into when not getting the proper assistance. They are wrecked, and not able to keep a steady job and have a career.   And then expected to do this while not eating food, or getting sleep. This leaves them to survive by depending on drug lords, or die.

Numbing and escaping reality is priority number one. This is where the opportunities of ignoring the conscience occur, and so betrayal becomes a norm to some, while others grumble and seek refuge. Because of this environment, there is vigilantism (the checkers). There are some who have a unique variable in the balance of empathy and apathy- where they see acts of cruelty that triggers an activism in them, to punish the evil doer with a brutal beating. So the undocumented empowerment is what really rules here, because they are subject to each other on a real level. This is usually their sole concept of justice. There's an ethic of mistreating women. Giget lost her bike, and it wasn't long before the perpetrator was getting his ass kicked for it. Once Doc Holiday slapped his girlfriend, and right after that he was smashed in the face with a baseball bat when he wasn't looking. Had to have reconstructive surgery. Genders are in competition with each other. For women, drugs are more attainable if you are more attractive to providers. Men strive for opportunities of drugs and sex. A lot of switching partners, though some remain. Many acts of violence are from the jealousy generated by this switching of partners. Everyone is trying to hold on to the smidgen they have, while it is escaping them. Camps are raided by both police, or other homeless. Seems impossible to have anything.

Beliefs- The common paradigm sees that society has discarded them, and that they are completely estranged from the stereotyping that they are a subspecies. They've been left in the dust, while society moves on without them. This is a general dynamic that goes on with whatever deity, or religion a person might favor. Most are their own versions of christian doctrines since their religion wasn't developed socially. Some are medlies of asian origins. Even the religions they may profess, have a certain take on it because they generally are excluded from the congregations of these religions and disciplines, which they see conform to the system that discards them. This is probably why so many of them make up their own beliefs and religions. Gorm professes Oden due to his nordic ethnicity. But overall, they see the oppression and cruelty, and it's very real in their lives, and no one seems to care.

Reflexivity- 51 years old, from the poor side of Downey California -old industrial south/west side of the town. Very rough environment. I grew up around violence, and drug abuse. My own substance abuse began at 10 years old. Homeless by 17, well educated in drug culture and familiar with the norms of delinquency. My homelessness started in 1985, and was a typical result of severe ptsd, and complex trauma. So the people on the streets sense my comfort and familiarity on the streets, and so there's no question as to me being ingenuine. They know I'm homeless, and sleep outside under a bridge. They sense my comfort on the streets, and we've seen each other in some pretty hard times. We've been there for each other in many ways in our attempts to survive. But there is one thing I notice that each of these groups have in common that I see something very significant; when they sense someone really cares, they usually respond. All those I document as examples of both sociopathic and psychopathic behavior, I have a peaceful understanding with. I treat them as they are; human beings created by God. I see them as victims of an antisocial society that treats them like objects, rather than people. They are made by the same God who made me, and so I can relate with the things that work in them. Without getting too close or involved, I treat them with respect, in a general way like we're all a part of the family of God's creation. I've even got to the point where I can only relate to people who've experienced the plight of chronic homelessnes and drug abuse due to

72

the result of a wrecked family, or child abuse. We are the only ones who understand how to be sensitive on certain levels. The streets are the only place you generally meet real people.

Smart-n-Final- I'm a regular customer and usually show up at night before bed, to get a little produce. But one morning I had to get to school, so I dropped in to see if I had money on my card. Glad to find the money was there, I started to shop and stopped to ask if I can have the combination to the bathroom. Lady tells me I can get the number on my receipt after I pay for the groceries. I ask "You mean I can't use the bathroom while I'm shopping? I've never heard that before and been a regular for the past 9 months." Manager comes and after hearing my wonder, says "the bathrooms are only for customers". I asked "so I'm not a customer until I give you my money? But I was shopping last night. So I can't use the bathroom?" He says "you can walk over to the McDonalds". I look at the cashier and she looks down at the floor. I show up a few days later at night when I usually go, and saw the cashier who usually checks me out. We are friends and have fun making each other laugh. I told her what happened and she said "WHAT!?, you are kidding me". When she realized I wasn't, she seemed troubled. The next night, we talked, but it wasn't the same. I could tell she felt estranged.

Frazier Farms- a very kind homeless man becomes friends with the employees of Frazier Farms. They all seem to love Sand-box who suffers from cancer and has to have a urine catheter that fell out one day and he had to go behind a dumpster stall to fix it when trying to urinate. He comes out and a security guard sees him and stops him saying "caught you." John tells him what he was doing, which he quickly learns from management he's not allowed at Frazier Farms anymore. This situation devastated John, who's still barred a year later.

McDonald's- The most unbelievable experience happened at McDonalds. Their employees were being abusive to the homeless, who would retaliate with messing up the bathrooms. Then the employees would retaliate by making life hell for all the customers by locking the bathrooms so you had to use a token to get in. They tell the homeless they have to be customers to use the bathroom, but not other people. So they have to go outside where it is illegal to go to the bathroom, and then be sighted by law enforcement who have a red carpet at every commercial bathroom in town. The very fact that police see their need for public bathrooms, but not the need for the homeless to have public bathrooms, and even criminalize them for going to the bathroom outside, demonstrates a severe level of demoralization of this society. Even the cruel Caesar's of Rome understood the basic need for public restrooms. I felt the employee wasn't cooperating with my attempt to use my EBT card there. When I asked to speak to the manager, she told me I have to leave. My friend and I looked at each other in shock. What??? She repeats the common dialogue, "we are a private corporation, we don't have to serve you." You can tell by their countenance, they like to say that to us.

Variables:

Radar- is in a perpetual state of grumbling about apathy. When dad was falling through the cracks, Radar was shocked the family was just going to let him be homeless, and leave him out there alone, so Radar went to go stay with dad. He's shocked at the level of dis-concern among family members. When dad died, he was left out there alone. Seems moral force of conscience led him to the streets. He's very trusting, and likes sharing. But he's a runt on the street, at the bottom of the pecking order, and a target for opportunism. He came down with spinal-meningitis and was rushed to the hospital, where he almost died. After almost a month in the hospital, he was released with atrophy so bad he could barely walk. A week later, he's repeatedly ticketed by a police officer for lying near a sidewalk. No mercy from a public servant. Apathy of police officer seems to be on a very extreme level. Roger told him over and over "I'm too weak to walk", and the policeman kept citing him when he was in need of assistance. The economy can't afford to support the needy, so now they are criminals. Somehow the rational mind of the officer has reached a level of fantasy that he's getting the bad guys. Seems to be on the level of hyper rational. Frightening to think a man with no regard for human life would have a gun and is licensed to kill. I guess they train them that way to make it easier to kill people. Sociopaths are generally hailed as the hero in this society, and the victims of their behavior are deemed as the criminals- those bad guys you pay money to keep in control.

Damen- very unstable, traits are that of severe levels of exposure. Has fits of rage over someone "fucking with his shit." Will impulsively charge at you when triggered.   Has moments of psychosis, extremely needy. After the episode he seems nice, though doesn't reconcile for behavior he's aware of. He hit a drunk in the back of the head with brass knuckles, who was sent to the hospital in critical condition.   Damen seems emotionally unaffected. Some of us will still give him food, because he lacks network. He's not so much part of us who share. He doesn't return favors when we give him food. Never really goes anywhere further than materialistic conversation; this stuff, that stuff.   From what I can tell, Damen has traits I recognize from working in foster care. Children who suffer severe levels of neglect have a particular spectrum and peculiarities. They are usually preoccupied by their gadgets and toys, and only pull away when a sudden urge comes to them.   In his mid 50s. I've watched him stand there with his basket of stuff, and then put a Robin stocking mask on his face while muttering something from his imagination. Later he grabbed a large tote found at the dumpster, and started swishing it through the water puddle making big water waves. He's very much an antisocial type, and has a capacity for extreme violence. This generally is a part of neglect; they develop methods of dominating in the strife for things. This can escalate into violence that becomes habit when unsupervised. Violations aren't followed up for moral programming. So he very much fits this in his routine, both putting other drunks in the hospital, and in return he ends up put in the hospital, often coming out with his head and limbs bandaged from severe wounds. But it's the way he goes about it, like an unruly toddler bully- the tyrant you don't want playing with your children. I've seen how this occurs from neglect. And how it results in not achieving social development because of this level of latency.   They end up trapped in this state they were in since they were a young child, and now into middle ages. A typical occurrence is in the baby of the family that came late, and then everyone was moved on and preoccupied with all the family matters and they end up totally overlooked. Many times, at vital developmental years, there's a family breakup and they're left with a traumatized parent who can't tend to the needs of the child, and is usually lost in some coping mechanism.

Sapphire- Was seen smashing a whiskey bottle in her boyfriend's face while he was sleeping. She's very hostile and sexually aggressive. She punches like a guy, with a feint, *"f*ck you!! I'll kick your fucking ass bitch!"* She has moments of psychosis like her boyfriend Kid, and so they share this relation, though he's quiet and keeps to himself. Like the other antisocial personalities, she lacks real conversation with anyone. Interaction limited to outbursts of anger, sexual arousal, hootin' and hollering, gimme mode, bash the ruling idiots. I had, -a couple of times- caught her at the right moment while she was coherent, and had a meaningful conversation with her about ptsd, and complex trauma, and how I learned why we self medicate. She shared a little about her experience, that she's all f*cked up because of some shit that happened when she was young. Her mom seems to blank out certain realities. The lack of confirmation from parents about serious pain has a devastating effect on the child.

These brief moments seemed to have meant something to her. I once stopped her from beating some lady up when I asked "hey Sapphire, what happened? Are you alright?" It threw her off, and she changed modes. Right after getting out of jail, she looked healthy and sober, and she came up to me and said "hey, I came back looking for friendship. That's what I'm here for". I sensed it was awkward for her not being her usual self, but she went through it anyone.

But Kid (her boyfriend) was there, so I wanted to be sensitive because she often makes him jealous. So I didn't respond the way I really wanted to. So it was awkward for me too, and she went back to habits, and I felt I let her down in some way. Once when it was during the cold of winter, Kid was attacked by someone with a machete who cut him across the top of his head. Kid got a hold of him and beat the shit out of him. The hospital sewed Kid up with about 20 stitches, and sent him right back out in the cold. This was one of two cases of machete attacks to the head that I saw during this short period.

Cletus- good ol' boy from Texas. Old and thin, he's still tough as nails. Enjoys nothing more than good conversation over a bowl of weed. Is generous to share the little that's left, and will go hungry not wanting to be a burden to us, but jumps at the offering of food. Sometimes rambles as if used to others not listening, but has much to say if ears are on. He shows much appreciation in attitude for the little things, even given the horrible conditions that he suffers. There are those of the anomaly that are sensitive in these simple ways. God bless them.

Merlin and Moomoo- Merlin was an old skateboarder from the 70's who used to own a bicycle shop on 101. He told me the way he ended up homeless, started when he noticed how success turned him into a hoarder. He said it really creeped him out. And so he lost his motivation for success, and he started just going out and sharing what he had and got lost in some scene on the street. At the time he ended up homeless, he got a little puppy he named Moomoo. When I met them on the streets of Oceanside, they had been on the streets for about 14 years. He would often have her riding on some makeshift bike trailer where she can sit and watch the adventure. Merlin became one of the caretakers on the street, helping those in need. He was generous to share what he had if you were really needy. He sometimes would know a young lady on the street from the time she was a little girl. And they would feel safe around Merlin. He has a real heart you can trust. I felt his reason for becoming homeless had to do with him wanting to preserve his conscience, to not adapt to selfish ambition. He doesn't have a lot of knowledge about these things. It's just a simple sense of moral conscience leading him.

Peer-support specialist model- When I started my work in counseling severe cases of ptsd and complex trauma during the nineties at the foster care facility in Escondido, and as a Stand-Up For Kids counselor for homeless teens and children in Oceanside, Psychotherapy wasn't quite fully developed at the time, reprocessing wasn't quite happening yet on an emotional level. Though we would try to help them reprecess things. My work was on a peer level of having severe trauma myself. Stand-Up specializes in this model that was established as the second tenet of trauma informed care. My work was unable to continue for my own need of reprocessing. After being removed from society for a time in a commune, and left at the end of 2018, I discovered the trauma informed care movement and went in for my own CEBT (cognitive emotional behavioral therapy). During my therapy, I was caught up to speed on psychotherapy and the developments in the technique, and saw room for growth.

I also discovered the research that was conducted in 2015 that started the movement, and backed up my experience working with the homeless. By scientific research, it was determined that chronic homelessness and substance abuse is all trauma related [Shelter from the Storm: Trauma Informed Care in Homeless Service Settings 2015]. 75 - 80 % were severe cases of child abuse- usually complex with molestations, and or beatings both physical and psychological. This backed up my experience working with the homeless, and hearing their pain, and seeing the psychological state they are in, and left in squalor. Many of these cases are abandonment, sometimes by both parents, and severe levels of neglect; If you could imagine the mind of a toddler left out in the cold to eat out of garbage cans. The other 20 - 25% are veterans, brain injuries cases which I found are usually victims of car accidents, some are cases of misfortune that lands them on the street -which in itself- is a serious ptsd event that can become complex given the conditions and demographics and influences within that environment. They usually do end up very complex with transference of molestations, and physical and psychological abuse, ect.

I developed my own peer support specialist model for ptsd and complex trauma. I became close friends with a psychotherapist at the wellness center, and right away confronted him with the plight of them having psychotherapy on their medi-cal insurance, that didn't include what had been determined scientifically; that they first need to have tenet 1 of trauma informed care; which is *safety and security*- a safe place to sleep with adequate vitals of food, water and medicine. This brings them out of the cycles between L1 (survival mode), and reverting to L2 for emotional release and coping. Tenet 1 stabilizes the complex limbic system, so they can come back to their senses and functionalities. This takes establishing a vital consistency. Next step from there is tenet 2; *peer support,* (someone who's been there and not above them), approached by someone who is trauma-informed within a sanitary environment that protects them emotionally and psychologically.

This is so a very special relationship can develop between the trauma survivor, and a trained psychotherapist they feel comfortable with. Sometimes it has to be the same gender association, sometimes the opposite. Healing only begins when achieving the tenet 3; *trust and transparency.* This is where the pain can come up, and be reprocessed in a *mutual collaboration-* tenet 4. Tenet 5 is *choice and empowerment* that charges them in their new hope they found when all the dots were connected in reprocessing their timeline during their 52 week period. This brings about corrective emotional responses displayed usually with constructive activism, rather than destructive activism. This is the confirmation of emotional and psychological healing. Psychotherapy is a method of accurately assessing the schema cognitively, and in that moment that they had brought you to, you help them process the right why. Reprocessing is so vital because in severe cases, the wrong why can totally fragment, and wreck a person's soul. Psychotherapy was originally a family function that has been removed from society that creates a private dilemma of being left to self process.

Sociology has proven that the individual perspective misses most of what's really going on, and needs cognitive confirmation by those near to them to put the right definition on actions when processing somatic (emotional) dilemmas. That is why in my model, I include a sociological perspective in this collaboration that takes away the direct impact on them personally, and adds a perspective that leads them to discover the impact on those who affected them, to see how they might have been hurt. This puts a healthy definition on these actions, and is essential for healing and moral reprogramming. This individual perspective is a psychological malady, produced by individualization that is paramount in this growing disability to rightly process. Processing is part of the social construct of reality. The need for CBT and CEBT is a breakdown of this construct. It's very simple- rational construct becomes social destruct. My model includes establishing a trauma informed services site, near where they choose to dwell. Reaching the vital tenet of trust and transparency is much easier when you are out there with them. They generally only feel comfortable with those who understand their plight and pain. There is a great chasm between the needy on the street, and the office at the psychotherapy and wellness center. My model was to meet them where they are at. Phase 2, is bringing those in the process of healing to farm hand cottages where they can learn to farm while they get their psychotherapy. This can end up in a barter support net.

statement- I contested the notion that they cannot receive healing by psychotherapy without first getting cleaned up and on pharmaceutical drugs. This initial approach already violates tenant 5, choices and empowerment, and disrupts the attempt at achieving trust and transparency they need for healing. This incentive comes from the criminalization of their coping mechanisms. Pharmaceutical entities have been the leading kingpin in turf war to sell drugs. So it is a force coming over them removing the ability of peer support. This authority coming over them has been a trigger for those betrayed by authority. This only causes them to relive this betrayal, and escape and revert to their choice of coping. These forces to conquer and dominate are the leading cause of homelessness and drug abuse. Those who are afflicted by the exposure are forced into self sufficiency when they are disabled from establishing a support network. And these forces demand to be the ones to deal with it. It is true that the mind has to be sober from certain substances for reprocessing. But this doesn't demand a clinical process of establishing certain chemical balances within your system. You do have to catch them when they are clear headed, and content to talk. The only need is that they are truly loved, and trust you enough to bring out the pain, but this is usually too agonizing for them.

Starchild- the most extreme level of ptsd and complex trauma I've ever seen. Antisocial level is to the point that she only lets her boyfriend into her world. Gorm is her link to the outside, and takes care of her, and is trusted with her access to assistance. He told me molestation started at 4 years old. She seems to have the deficits that come from severe neglect. Her norms are extreme. She's exposed herself publicly without the estrangement she feels when she cries out loud like an infant. She lacks remorse for how she affects him.

Gorm's story seems to be a typical betrayal that orphans experience, they are devastated by the realization they're not really part of the placement family. Both Starchild and Gorm are addicted to opiates. He's expressed a desire to get clean, and he said she has expressed that to him in the past. Case is very complicated because she won't talk to others unless in desperation for food or drugs. He told me she just suddenly slipped into psychosis. I wonder if it could've involved an altering of imagination by euphoria, with almost no cognitive interaction. Cognitive confirmations of reality are almost non-existent. She's a special case, because her apathy is from severe trauma and neglect, lacking the moral development one needs for conscience. Needs tremendous investment, as for an infant at her age. She was my initial inspiration to bring trauma informed care to the street because her case is so severe. She couldn't be forced to be in a clinic, but had to be met where she is.

I felt she would come out of her psychosis if she had a place that she felt safe, a healthy reality to fall into. I had been going on this effort of establishing a social construct of reality with her through cognitive interactions that were normal, and caring. The effort was bleak and relying on a miracle from God. Because of her psychosis, it got to the point of Gorm becoming her sole connection to the outside world; a level of dependency that had horrifying consequences for her. He got to where he wasn't able to withstand the load of her neediness, and started to ditch her. This would hit the devastating wound of abandonment, and she would run aimlessly screaming in agony "where are you!!?" This became unbearable for me,,, sometimes she would scream in terror for hours. He would periodically return and she would go through the entire agonizing process all over again. After a couple weeks, she found new ways of survival. It was a difficult transition for her, but she seemed to really need It. It forced her by sheer survival to develop a support network. This was a strange period for her. Her imagination was affecting her appearance. She would wear the most ridiculous combinations of articles of clothing. Sometimes she would come out looking like a scary bug. She would sometimes buy costumes when she got money, and act out plays in her head. And in her interactions with these fictitious characters you could see an amazing amount of creativity and talent. She once played a character in a Broadway Musical dressed in a purple and gold top-hat suit with a cane she got from the costume store downtown. Character and play was all part of her psychosis.

Camp on Wheels- one night me and Sandbox were walking over on south oceanside blvd and stopped to look at a patch of M1 dirt. I asked him if it would be a good spot for another rock garden. That night we mapped out a little plan. I had a section to do a little miniature creek that spilled into miniature pools. Sandbox was the first one on it the next day. That's why I call him Sandbox. I went to the city library and accessed the GIS map to check on that ¼ mile strip along South Oceanside Blvd. Turned out to be public utility. As far as I knew, there was no law prohibiting the homeless from being on public property. Laws that did apply, only pertain to blocking walkways, and unsightliness. This strip was only dirt, and no obvious point of destination. Road was usually a place for truckers to park for rest and access to establishments. I began working on a plan to establish a trauma informed service site there. I engineered a system you can roll out of a storage in the evening, quickly set it up, sleep, and roll away in the morning to stay in the storage during the day. I felt this would give a sense of having a safe place to sleep. I also engineered a chuck wagon that you can roll out, cook a quick meal, and roll back into the storage. So this would now stabilize them to be able to function and get processing.

And even part time work at the temp agency. I have a knack for cooking, and loved making them good tasting healthy food that was hardy. This communicates they are important, and that you appreciate them. It also puts a little salve on the wound. This all has to be from genuine care for them, understanding their plight and desiring that they be healed. There were some who got the most in on the cooking, because they just happen to be around during those times. Schedule irregularity proved both these efforts to be a difficult task. I started to use the camp system in oct of 2019, it was unusually wet during this time. The tent system has to be above ground, so I engineered a system of a single person tent fixed on a cot with an attachment that left out the need to use rope and spikes. So you could quickly set it up on the sidewalk if needed, and it wouldn't be a problem. The spot I started was on the sidewalk easement next to where me and John were working on the rock garden.

It was at this time that some of the homeless went to the man who was driving around in a truck pulling a shower trailer (Jordan Verdin and *Humanity Showers*). He came and filmed a demonstration of the first Camp on Wheels prototype. It was he and other associates of his that brought awareness and support to my efforts. It was Jordan's heart to give the poor a voice by posting their testimonies on his instagram. He also takes their pictures with professional equipment and makes them look like rock stars. After a while, John's effort was making it a beautiful spectacle, with even a small pumpkin patch with stakes of old wood making it look like a spot on a ranch. People were constantly expressing appreciation for the scenery and art. But the landscapers took it upon themselves when discovering this wonderful spectacle, to destroy all the beauty, most of what was John's hard labor. He hung a sign there that simply asked "Why This"? Even a sheriff was disgusted with the mess they left of what was once beautiful. He thought there should be media exposure to this situation. John was broken hearted, and took what he wanted of the stones, and left the rest. It became my own little project of restoration and re-beautification next to where I slept every night.

Senior Pepe'- is sensitive. He was the first one to become a regular resident. His first night was met in the morning with a rude awakening by a gang of police officers. I questioned the attitude of the leading officer who seemed to be taking an obvious enjoyment in bullying homeless people. I asked him how he was raised, and he gave much honor and appreciation for the good parenting he received from his parents. I said "well that's very wonderful your parents were good with you. But I think your maker would want you to have mercy and compassion on those not so fortunate as to end up with good parenting." He started to become contentious in such a way, someone was having to counsel him on his mobile cb headset. The incident made it so we had to move from the corner of the street, down a ways by the storage. Senior Pepe remained as a regular and worked at jobs and got psychotherapy and even became a contributing member of Camp on Wheels. He became my partner in setting up tents:

Once he was raging about someone stealing his stuff. I told him "all our stuff -to God- is a big pile of shit. He looks down and sees us fighting over shit. We don't realize how important we all are." I was stunned by his response; he started to cry and confess how he was putting stuff over people. He said "God please have mercy on me, I need to be saved." Not even aware of the sinner's prayer, he demonstrated a true contrite heart, and a cleansing of his conscience by confession, and repentance, and a desire to turn from his ways. He likes the idea of sharing, and trusts others even when it might be considered unwise. He goes through fits of anger, because it's so hard to find someone trustworthy. It's become a very deep wound for him. I discovered something in one of our sessions, he seems to have the social conflict from an impaired right temporal lobe. This kind of impairment can wreck a person's family because of wrong processing of the deficit.

Starchild awakenings- After a year of supporting her regularly with vitals, and caring for her wounds and need for warmth. She began to have awakenings at the campsite. First time she came to me there and said with coherent words "I think I need to get some help". I was astonished by her presence, it was as if I was meeting her for the first time. She was suddenly there, and talking normally. I said "are you going to do everything you need to do?" She nodded, and started to walk away, and I said "well I'll be your friend. I'll even go with you to the wellness center if you want." She stopped, and took another drag of her cigarette, and stood there for a moment, and then walked away. I noticed with severe cases of neglect and trauma, that they create fantasy when they are faced with emotional situations they can't process, they create a fantasy in which to escape the moment. When trauma becomes routine, this becomes a programmed method of escape when they are triggered emotionally. They get lost in this altered state, by the continual avoiding of the brutal reality. They can be rescued from this psychosis if genuine love and concern create a healthy and safe reality to fall into.

Starchild continued to have these awakenings. Right after that, there was another moment when she came to the camp for water. I was stunned when after I gave her the money to get something to drink, she held up her arms for a huggy, and after a nice brother sister hug, she turned to me and asked "are you thirsty, would you like me to get you something to drink?" I was taken back, I said "no, I'm fine, thank you." She pointed at Doc Holliday and asked "can he go with me cuz they wont let me in the store.?" I sent Mike to go with her in case the store manager didn't let her in. Doc Holiday, said "what the fuck was that? I ain't never seen her talk normal like that." I was in a state of shock because of her normal interpersonal interaction that entertained a thought for me, that would take up some of the five dollars I gave her. After that day, Gorm came back from being gone for a while, and I told him about the awakenings. He was intrigued and went to find her. When I caught up with him later, he affirmed the awakening and stated "she totally came out of it without anti psych meds' '.

The real change came after she went to jail for a few weeks for attacking Gorm with a five foot piece of rebar. When she got out, she was clean and her face filled in and healthy. But she sat there on the grass looking hungry. So I went and got her breakfast. When I came back, I saw what she had put on, and I scolded her. She was only wearing see-through panties, and high heels with a tee shirt. After giving her the food, I said "put some pants on, and take those stoopid shoes off." "Baby girl is NOT a sex toy!!" As I walked away I repeated, "baby girl is not a sex toy!." About an hour later, I was cooking, and she walked right by me wearing a very nice levi skirt that went down past her knees, and a knitted cotton blouse. No high heels. I said "wow, that is more like it". "You look very nice." From that moment on, she remained in the awakened state, and was her old bratty self. She even had moments where I saw shame on her face, after I asked "how are you doing." She could hardly look at me, and her countenance was as if she was upset suddenly. But she was clear minded, and healthy.

The next time I saw her, she was nicely dressed and walking down the street next to another girl and they were talking like they were friends. I asked those who have known her since a child, and this was very different for her. She now started covering herself, and continuing to develop cognitively. She got to a point of reacting to her level of dependency on me, and not knowing who I was. Gorm explained a little. She wanted to use me to make him jealous, but didn't understand why I supported her but had no sexual interest in her. She thought I would get jealous. I told her once, I don't help you because you have a vagina. God made you, and he wants you to be loved. After that, we became like friends. She loved our normal conversations, and got to the point where she would create these fictitious scenarios to engage in mock intellectual conversations. She would sit a certain way with her cigarette, as if she's portraying a sexy character in a movie. So I would engage in this for development. She has an amazing imagination. I've watched her slowly come out of her psychosis more and more. We now talk in reality, rather than made up conversations. This is an oedipus stage of development. At some point, she must have receded in her development.

We had a guest who was going rogue on us. He stopped cooperating to break down the equipment, and just started building on what I was lending him, and was reluctant to consider our plea to not ruin it for all of us. We knew if we didn't break it down for the day, it would bring a lot of heat on us. There were only four or five of us at the time. This was a little more than a year after I had first started setting up on this strip. After a few weeks, he was still not getting any of the tickets for staying set up all day. Soon it was clear, the biggest obstacle in this effort to stabilize them, was having a place where they could store their stuff. The strip didn't quite become what I intended until I used a small 6 x 4 canopy that I would leave all the way down, and hang black mover blankets as walls to cover the inner space. This was first my idea for a summer suit that was more ventilated and cooler during warmer temperatures.

I was growing tired of turning away people who needed to leave their stuff for someone to watch. This can be a means of ending up stranded for hours. One day, store managers were disturbed by one of the homeless laying right off the sidewalk, it was Pig Pen with all his trashy looking stuff. After he awoke, he asked if I could watch his stuff, knowing he needed to be freed up to make his runs, I got the idea to set up one of the canopies along the strip to hide his stuff underneath. He was so excited after that, he took off on his bike "thanks Rodney!, now I can make it to recycling." It suddenly dawned on me- he now had social mobility and security. At this point I was giving in and leaving the tents up because the rains were making it difficult to break down and set up and keep everyone's bedding dry. At the time I set up the storage unit for Pig Pen, two others noticed the situation, and I had enough canopies so I set two more up that night. By the end of the next week, I had a third of the street lined up with tents and storage units. 12 tents, and 6 units. This was it, it was happening, it was becoming a trauma informed service site. Some of my supporters who were involved with serving the homeless started raising money on their own to contribute. Before I knew it, I had a team working hard to meet the growing need for more tents and storage units. Some of those I was taking care of joined in the effort to keep the street and parking lots impeccable. Those who were accustomed to leaving disasters were respecting the effort, and not making it harder for us. What helped that was hearing their pain, and validating it.

Lilly was one who would come hang out in that general part of town, and by the time she left the next day, the place she hung out at was a total disaster area. And in the midst of the catastrophe, she was always faithful to leave a little bouquet of flowers. Lovely flowers.. One morning she caught me cleaning it all up. When she approached me I said "good morning". She then started to explain her motives, the message to the cops and the establishments. It all came from very deep emotional pain and suffering. After validating her pain, I simply said "I don't think they're really getting your message. I think they're too dumb to understand your deep thoughts and your valid point." She started saying she was sorry and began helping me clean up the mess. Later when she came for a day, the spot she hung at near the camp with her cart and bags, remained relatively clean. And then when she left, she cleared the few things there, and the only thing she left was the bouquet of flowers. Lovely flowers. Just a little bit of caring and a miracle from God happens. It doesn't take super heroes, it just takes caring.

One night around midnight, an older homeless man showed up with a cart of cans, and laid down a small mat and sleeping bag to sleep near where my tent was stationed in between the hospitality canopy and one of the guest tents. The next morning, the man was gone. But earlier that evening, he showed up and started nestling where he stayed the night before. I approached him and introduced myself. He said something like "well I saw what was going on in the new papers, and decided to make it over here to see if I could fit in". There was something so pleasant about him, and familiar. His accent was the same as my mom's side of the family in Vermont, and when I told him, he lit up and asked "what part of Vermont?" So I told him Winooski, and he said out loud "I come from just the other side of the river near Boston." We talked a long time, and I set him up right away with a tent and a storage unit for his cans. The manager from the storage place said it was starting to look like a small town. She told me I should think of a name for the town. After telling one of the guests, he said "yeah, something like 'Fallville.'" I said "wow, it's like a place where we fall." It was the perfect name. I noticed something about my new friend from Boston -Mr Hensley, he was a sensitive man. What was notable about him was the correlation of his sensitive conscience, and his group orientedness, and an uprightness that doesn't really find much common ground around here. He actually works by travel, but he's a minimalist, who recycles to get just the little food, and a bottle of soda. He doesn't drink alcohol or do any drugs, just loves to talk about the ball game. He's very social in the sense of sharing in the hunting and gathering. He's also done some research for a University if I remember correctly. He immediately became a team player, bringing me all the updates going on with the city council, and the newspaper articles. So much so that I declared him the official Representative of Fallville. This was to go along with the joke around town that I was the Mayor. I think we both got a little sense of home being neighbors. We had shared many meaningful conversations, and moments during our stand against the forces of darkness. It could also be seen in his moral makeup, that he had no tolerance for the way people disrespect each other around here. I also have the same struggle. He definitely had a trigger- a wound that is deep. He would get loud like I do, and then after his rant, he would grumble how he's not such a nice guy like the rest of us. His realness and sincerity was so refreshing, you could want to kiss the old bearded man. And it was hard to remember his yelling; it showed he had a strong moral force in him. And he was like grandma; they are the kind of people who are faithful to pay back every cent.

Slowly more and more people were coming and sharing their pain, and I was able to help them process some of the most devastating things that could happen to people. You could see the healing in process- the emotional release when certain things were explained to them, and an immediate change in behaviors. One case was a young man I called obed. After staying a while and being part of the team, we had a very intense session about his father. It all came down to a disruption in attachment that needed to be reprocessed. That Christmas he was able to be with the family, and I got an amazing report after. He immediately sobered up and ended up getting a stable job and place to stay. I was very proud of him. He is the champion of his healing, because he trusted with very deep pain, and responded with what was truly in his heart already. We all just need the pieces put back together. None of us can do it alone. Obed participated in finding that mutual collaboration, and was just receptive to what came to him. It was amazing at the end of the session when I was able to reprocess some of my own pain that I shared with Obed. Just his care and participating in our collaboration, helped me find some things that weren't quite processed right. We share this special moment.

One day a man comes to me and says, "hi, I'm looking for Rodney". I said "here I am". He said "nice to meet you. I am Gary Warth from the *Union Tribune*, may I do an interview with you". I said "sure". We talked for about an hour, and then he left. The next day he showed back up and had a photographer take some pictures and he asked more questions. That Sunday an article was on the front page of the local section. I was astonished, and excited that he explained my formula for my model. A couple of days after that, people started coming to me, "hey Rodney." I saw your face on the front page of the google web-site. I said "what? Google?" "Yeah, I turned on my phone, and saw your face." The next thing I heard later was people saying the article was in the Los Angeles Times. And then other small newspapers, even some from small towns. I wasn't so much a cyber surfer, so I passed it off as in keeping with the many demands coming my way.

Time Ghost- was the new kid in town. He was the subject of some of the blame-game when shit turns up missing. That's always how it is for the new kid in town, they get blamed for shit missing, and suddenly have enemies taxing them. We clashed at first, because he had a stark opposition to the concept of God. When on the spiritual subject, he would go into great detail about his discovery that answered everything. He first spoke of things he experienced that would indicate cognitive dissonance, mentioning the feelings of guilt, and discontent with the state of the world, and explained that this caused him to think there was something wrong with him. Then said his epiphany set him free from all those concerns. But those things he explained, were the kind of things that could be expected to suffer given reasonable concern.

It's almost like he was explaining just detaching from it all. Which I can see to a certain point. But it seemed it was to the level of being complacent with everything, rather than just finding peace despite you suffering over it. There's something about the moral force of our conscience, it will cause us to suffer because we care. He insisted I consider his complicated epiphany, but I didn't like the place it led him to, which was not doing anything about anything. If we stand for everything, then we stand for nothing. I would rather suffer while maintaining whatever God put in me to care. What I found interesting, was he swore to have discovered the secret to all the entire universe, and that no one has ever discovered it before, and the whole universe has lacked this great acknowledgement. But then he demanded me realize that I was extremely egotistical and arrogant for not believing him.

One of the first significant participants was a retired Fire Department Paramedic; Eagle Eyes, who immediately swooped in with excitement saying he'd been trying to do what I was doing for a long time. I guess he was trying to work with an unworkable city. He told me how he saw people dying of things on the street that were very simple to handle if someone was there at the time. He wanted there to be clinical care right on the street. You could see how we shared a lot of the same sentiments and feelings about the system, and its apathy towards those who suffer. One morning he showed up with a truck load of mulch, fresh mulch from red wood. He said it was good for the septic in the M1 soil that we were camped on. So we spread it around all the tents making it look very much like a small neighborhood. It gave a very clean and orderly look to our little town. This was bringing a sense of being part of the community. We were out there, some of those in our camp, with shovels and rakes while Eagle Eyes dropped load after load until we covered almost the whole ¼ mile length of the street.

We had a problem with Starchild, she had dislocated her hip, but would not let anyone with badges near her. It had been weeks, and it was dire she got her hip put back in place. I tried to get Paul involved, but it was against some of his oaths. But I differed because of her lack of mental capacity to discern the need for assistance. But he didn't give up on it so quickly. We kept trying to find a way. He showed up one morning, and as we talked at his tail-gate, Time Ghost came over and asked for water. He said he felt really strange. Five minutes later, me and Eagle Eyes saw him laying out on the side-walk. Eagle Eyes runs and grabs his triage kit to check his vitals, and comes back to tell me he's rushing him to the hospital- his blood pressure was dangerously low. He shows up a day later, and tells me that Time Ghost almost died in the hospital. His pneumonia had gone septic, and became an infection that demanded

emergency blood transfusion. The doctor said if Eagle Eyes wasn't there, Time Ghost would have died. He was still in the hospital for several days, and then his mom came to pick him up and took care of him for a little while. Eagle Eyes was eager, and went to the city to try and get some cooperation with waste management, but the city was reluctant to help in any way. He got the idea to purchase some land in Oceanside, and have me work with him there, where I would hold down the fort on the social side, and he would be there for medical assistance. Soon we had half the street lined up, and more money coming for more equipment. One morning a total media frenzy showed up at the camp. Two news networks came at different times. Another phenomenon of people driving up all day, opening their trunks and dropping off goods. We suddenly realized the traffic was constantly going down the road. We never saw that much traffic on that small street before. Cars drove by us all day long with their phones pointed at the camp. City council members, and people from housing and other departments of the city, came with questions. People from several organizations with more questions and business cards. One family drove up, and brought out all this specially catered food all the way from Orange County. More news networks started showing up. Even some from media networks and cable networks. I began having to turn a lot of things away because we didn't have the room to store it all. And the dumping was messing up the cleaning effort. I became a slave to this all day everyday. I could have filled a warehouse with the things I had to turn away.
I even set up a pick up from contributors who looked to find room to store things. I was also getting a lot of hateful people showing up to let us know what a bunch of scumbags we are.

By another couple of weeks, we had the whole ¼ mile strip lined up with about 30 tents and 20 6 x 4 canopy storage units. We all started really having a sense of community, and family. People started pressuring each other to help do their part. People were more involved in healthy ways that had to do with taking care of each other. We only had a couple of veterans, but there was a wide range of different personas. Even one resident who didn't drink or do any drugs. Some were just casual pot smokers or light drinkers. I generally couldn't take care of cases with heavy alcohol use because I wasn't set up for a wet tent system. The couple cases that did end up at the camp, was because of their level of de-abilitation from brain damage. One was a paraplegic who was paralyzed on one side of his body. He was left for dead on the sidewalk down the street. The other one was a serious case of diabetes that left him hardly able to walk with a walker and a backpack. This social engineering was the biggest challenge. You can't just have anyone sleeping next to anyone. There has to be given an equal amount of space between tents and storage units. And there's certain types that go well together, and certain types that don't. And they have certain schedules, so I had to separate the schedule zones. Some abused women wanted to stay near other women. Most wanted to be woven in among the other men for safety issues.

Starchild's christmas party- there was something kind of haunting that happened that fits into the category of 'unexplainable.' One time, when Starchild was in a certain frame of mind, it seemed like God would talk to me through her in a little ways. There was something so important I had forgotten all about, and God reminded me. I was so proud of Starchild for the overcoming she did during the year, I wanted to give her a Christmas party where me and Merlin and 9-52 would give her presents to open wrapped with Christmas paper so she could tear them open. We all kept it a secret so it would be a surprise. I had totally forgotten about it until one night she came late to my tent, and walked back and forth in front of my tent saying as if not knowing if I'm in there, "honey boy, honey boy, mommy was supposed to get some presents. When's mommy going to get her presents honey boy?" And then she walked away. She was in a very low state of awareness, and I checked and found out no one told her. How did she know about the presents? It was so spooky, the way she was saying it. Not having normal cognitive socialization, she generally doesn't ever greet someone by saying their name. She'll know who they are by hearing their name, but she doesn't socialize in that way. After a long time of helping her, honey boy is the only name she ever called me. Her reminder was just in time for me to get the presents wrapped and ready for the little party. The coloring book and pen set was her favorite one.

The media I guess was getting pretty intense about the situation, and I was hearing a lot of things here and there. One common theme was that somewhere in these forums, there was support to give Rodney the money to deal with the homeless. I laughed so hard. This is where things got real hot. Suddenly the city wasn't so nice about it. It was like they went to war or something. On the 23 of march, there was a police raid at one of the tents near the end of the block. Punky Darla told me the officers just popped his head into the tent where she laid there with her boyfriend in bed. I was shocked and very upset. The most common detriment that leads them to life on the streets on drugs, is authority violating privacy. It is a devastating wound that fragments moral structure. It seemed to be an obvious case of breaching an expectation of privacy. Plus, from the beginning it was established that these are my tents I'm sharing with my friends. So I can keep them there and in certain conditions. Law is they have to come to me before entering. All that was confiscated was illegal search and seizure.

The next morning on March 24, I was a witness to a police raid four tents down from me. I watched the police officer walk up to a large tent, unzip the doorway, and pop his head in, breaching an obvious expectation of privacy at around 8:00 in the morning. After the raid, they found out they had the wrong tent. The person they were looking for, lived in the tent next door, and wasn't even there at the time. That same day around noon, I was walking back from the showers and when I was next to McDonalds, I could see an officer just going into one of the tents with the main occupant at the side of the door where they were talking. I scolded the officers for completely abandoning the protocol for due process. Their response was that a customer at the coffee shop saw someone through the window with a pipe. So just going on a call, police have free reign to barge their privacy. To a trained psychotherapist, the most critical pressing need is protection of their privacy. It can be expected that violating their privacy would trigger them and cause them to increase coping mechanisms. Becomes a risk of overdose.

Sure enough, that night began overdoses with those who were dependent on opiates. I was part of reviving some of them. I had trained certain members, the procedure for administering Nar-can, nasal mist. It reopens plugged receptors that block memory for breathing. All have to be trained, and there has to be control on the supply. I was glad for the training, it was the first time during the camp that we had a succession of overdoses. This went on for two days, and involved around seven cases of revival. Starting that night on the 24th of March, and carried on to the 25th, and 26th. About half included paramedic assistance. They were amazingly able to just drive up to a certain tent, and begin immediate assistance. The usual routine would be driving around the parking lot, and or looking around the creek. Opiate overdoses need immediate assistance to avoid brain damage from lack of oxygen.

That afternoon, a port-a-potty service drove up to deliver two units on the campsite. A wonderful man from a church came and told us his church wanted to donate them to us for safe sanitation. We were so excited. And then suddenly the HOT Team showed up (Homeless Outreach Taskforce). Officers stopped the delivery, and stated it was because of codes. So I asked them if they had the number for code enforcement, and they told me "no." When we looked into it, there was no code for it. It was simply private property on public property. If the city insists, there can be a written letter. But there was no law prohibiting us from having port-a-potty service. This was an undocumented empowerment without legitimate order to hinder our attempts to survive in a safe and humane way. This was at the same time the owner for the property of the stores across the street was locking all the trash can stalls so we couldn't throw away our trash. So then the trash started to pile up. And we had nowhere to put it. This was creating a biological hazard. The HOT Team was on the news the next day explaining how the camp had to move because there's no waste management or port-a-potty service, right after they turned them away the day before.

Another important engagement was that of a non-profit that builds farm hand cottaging. They offered to build cottages for me if I could find some land. So I connected him to the Housing Dept. who offered possible alternatives to move the camp to another location. The report I got from the organization was that we had the ok to build on the old abandoned high school property, and that the Mayor gave the ok for me to run it. This was quickly shot down by mister big money. He's one of three members who see no real need for the other members of the city council, who all just kind of go along with whatever the money says we got to do, they don't even have to live in our city. Everyone is trying to avoid the obvious blatant bullying that is going on in public office. When Eagle Eyes had got the property to do what we planned, he got resistance from the bullies despite what other council members would say, or even the citizens of Oceanside. The bullies said "trust us", 'we got 11 properties to work with, we'll find something. Just don't let them move on to your property.' I had a council member right there on the site, telling me about two properties they had where we were going to be able to go. They just had to "work out some bureaucratic stuff." This was as they were trying to get us into accepting vouchers to move off the sight. This is right at the time he is trying to sell me on the voucher idea. I told him point blank; you are just wasting all the money if they are just put in boxes and you cut off their ability to have access to peer support. White coats only further estrange them. The second tenant of trauma informed care is peer support. That fact itself, is saying that the real potential for success in the field of psychotherapy to heal masses of people on the streets is recruiting those out there in it. They have the heart, and already know by their own pain and suffering, how to be sensitive to those suffering that level of hurt. I have seen them, but didn't have the facilitation. What I created, was totally destroyed leaving me out there with nothing all over again. People have to understand that just giving them their shelter and food and needs is not the pressing need according to what research has determined. The pressing need is emotional, there are 'why's' that have to be established. There needs to be healing in a sanitary healing environment, but not in a white room with black curtains at the station. They need it in a natural habitation with trees and plants outside, where they are with nature and having the will right there in front of their cottage. Beds of kale and chard right there with free instruction on farming, and agriculture. I have a homeless lady friend, who is disabled in a wheelchair stuck in a room that racks up money that she is now stranded in, and needs to escape to find a reason to go on. She would love to be able to seed stacks of starter trays to be planted in a garden as she's sitting in her wheelchair. But her room is far from these things, and people just tell her she can do mail order assembly by herself in the solitary confinement that has already been determined to cause severe levels of psychological suffering by Gracen at Harvard University. I'm a trained farmer. I could be doing all this if I had a farm. Or farms. I was sending some of my guests to the Psychotherapy and Wellness Center already in the process of healing where the therapist was able to continue where I left off in the timeline. I could see how many of these young men and women out in the streets would make amazing psychotherapists because of their inside knowledge of the underworld and the plight of survival. Three wanted to get involved and so already had begun their own detox which has proven to be effective for them in the past. It's not that none of them can ever get off it, it's just they generally have nothing else in their life to keep them off it.

This is where the gospel comes in, and calls everyone to give up everything, and lay it at the feet of those serving the needs to the neediest. Does the orphan need a fish? Or does he need someone to take him fishing? In this, a family is born and a will is given to the orphan and widow to teach them how to fish, instead of just giving them a fish. The hard lesson learned in the family I was in was that if you try to do Acts 2 and 4 in some other way, it will end up wicked. The point of the money at the feet of a man in rags, was that it was the opposite of bowing to the money. That is worshiping mammon; bowing to the money. People should want the money to be in the hands of those who genuinely care, rather than just those who are better at getting it. But then those who care, are better at discerning needs versus wants and that's where it all goes downhill from there for those who think wants should be on the needs list.
There is a real problem in special interests with having money in the hands of those of moral fiber. There's nothing to work with when they are trying to lobby for their corrupt agendas. (Oh no, he's that guy who yells about all the shit I'm getting away with). The majority take the path that leads to destruction, so the sociopath is always going to win the election. Because one of moral fiber is among the few who genuinely care, and have strong moral values. So enter through the narrow gate, for wide is the gate to destruction.

After we were moved into the Motel, I told the case Management about what I was told. And so this left us hanging. After no response, I began to inquire about getting a response from the housing dept, in which he suddenly disappeared and wouldn't answer his phone. He was right there on the sight, but now for a week he was gone. I wasn't able to get a response from the council. I discovered that some of my residents from the camp were still left there with no voucher. One of them was a very serious case of abandonment, which he had to suffer again. And you could see it in him, he suffered from how he was dealt with. My camp was a trauma informed service site that was invaded by criminalization that caused further detriment to them emotionally and psychologically. This continued on in the motel that they sent us too. We were all expected to stay in our rooms and not have guests. I wasn't even allowed to do my peer support. I wasn't able to know who's coming or going. They were sent places without me knowing where they were going. Many were kicked out without me even knowing what happened. We were totally denied our rights socially. Couldn't even have family or friends come visit. You could hang out in the front outside the building for a smoke. But I was pressured by management to not hang out around there. Then I was given an evacuation notice two weeks before the time we were promised. I finally found out that the very council member who was making all these promises, totally shot down my whole thing without me even being there to refute it. He was making it off like he was going to try and help us, and then came against those who supported us. He pulled the ol "*bait-and-switch*" on homeless people. I wasn't even able to say anything or even know about it. This was heartbreaking, because we were excited about the new plans that included the land to farm on, and the cottaging building crew who were ready to build some shelters for us. I was trying to give them hope, and was totally duped in it. That is why we are stuck, because we have no representation while we are plundered. We aren't desirable for regulated employment. So we try to work under the table for side jobs, and don't get paid what we are owed. It is even written in ancient scripture, about those who owned fields who overworked the poor, and did not pay them what they owed. Money isn't a fair game, many get betrayed to the point of ruin. Most of those betrayed are probably children at the time of betrayal. This was also a blow to Eagle Eyes, who for so long dreamed of having a place where we who care could watch over them while we help them. He watched people die on the streets needlessly by simple things that could have been dealt with if someone was there.

Dough Boy- could tell right away he was a head injury case by soft cranial deformation, indicating an injury during the time the skull was still soft. When I asked, he said he injured his head when he was three years old. I detected some deficits right away that pointed to probable right and left temporal lobe. There were signs of the left temporal ADD, and he also had a problem with boundaries and norms on the subconscious level. According to Dr. Amen's case studies, this would indicate possible damage to the right temporal lobe. Neuro-feedback was his recommendation. It is a technological way of training certain parts of the brain, to do what the damaged part of the brain used to do. Very expensive, and not included in Medical Insurance. I also detected probable frontal lobe damage that might have included a disengagement in the emotional somatic circuit at the mpfc. He had an obvious cognitive impairment that was different from just the oversimplified structure of neglect. But he would say certain words that gave clues to what he's trying to communicate, as if there were problems with word finding, this is another indication of damage to the left temporal lobe. His normal state of mind was over simplified, but almost shut down. Without drugs, he would just stand there, and look around. Ask for a cigarette, or something to eat. Smoking pot would just get him fat from the munchies. But when he ended up on stimulants, he would suddenly become erratic and impulsive, and dangerously unstable. On an impulse he would turn and hurl a steel pipe in a random direction. This made people feel very uncomfortable with his presence. I wasn't able to set him up at the camp. Some of them were afraid of killing him. So I would set him up out of sight on the fringe of the underground camp area." Though people would react so to him. At times he was chilled out. He would try to be friendly, and say "what's up dog". Although he was high functioning in consideration of brain injuries, he was not adequately able to network in a way you need to survive on the streets. His mother came looking for him to see if I was setting him up, and I told her I wasn't able to at the camp, and that he disappeared after a run in with some of my guests. It was too tempting for him to come hang out. I felt bad. Some were threatening to hurt him. They don't understand him. I was afraid he would get killed. And so I told his mom, "I'm afraid if your son doesn't get off the streets, he's going to get killed. He doesn't understand the way he violates others." I later found out his mother became worried, because the programs would not let him stay. No matter who or where. Right after being thrown out of a facility he just checked into, he ended up dead 24 hours later. He was found five miles away from where he normally would be. This is a sign of being ostracized and banished from the area. Here's where the structure we are forced to depend on in our liberation, doesn't really have much incentive to help our needy family members when they are disabled. No common life, no common interests. They can care less how this society torments the soul.

People were way above us knowing what was going on in the situation. Activist groups started showing up. One was a Native American group. I forgot his name, but I remember his spirit that sent a message he had printed on the back of his shirt, the words- "You Are On

Stolen Land." This resonated with me because of my personal feelings about how the natives were treated. We could both relate to our land being taken by force by those who conquer the land and all its resources, and toss you out in the process. I felt humbled by his presence, and was greatly honored that he was there supporting and protecting the cause God put in my heart. I would hope to lay down my life and die for such people. These groups were stationing themselves across the street of the camp on a 24 hour watch. They were communicating to us and keeping us up to date with what the city was doing. And so I passed it on and we were ready when the police came with evacuation notices. Michael McConnel from twitter was very informative, and a powerful influence in confronting the city on their official website, and communicating their vague inconsistent responses that didn't look good.

Punky Darla's boyfriend Risk had died of a Fentanyl overdose shortly after we were moved out of our camp. They were the first ones raided on our site. I had witnessed myself what Punky explained about the officer just poking their head right in the tent where they were laying together. I witnessed this the very next morning with the second raid that happened a few tents down from mine. This is a very serious act against someone who has been violated. To anyone who is trained in psychotherapy, and I myself can attest by the many cases of trauma that I've helped, the most common detriment that would contribute to the said 'cause' of chronic homelessness and drug abuse, would be the violation of privacy by authority. It comes down to authority violating privacy– that is the big kahuna that makes up most of the cases out here. And so a very serious trigger can be expected when this wound is hit again, and they suffer by reliving it. Among all the things that led to Risk's demise, that was definitely in the line-up of the probable causes. Terrorists have many colors, and even uniforms nicely creased and brandishing a shiny badge. To a boy who grew up with real monsters in his life, where you couldn't just turn off the television to make them go away, police officers are just part of the long line of monsters that have been attacking them and criminalizing them for their emotional instabilities that they don't even understand. Emotions are probably the most difficult force to understand, and know how to control. And the boy is just supposed to get it together, and get his butt making money? People cracking them with the whip to get on the assembly line, is part of the nightmare that they aren't worth anything if they don't have money. Anyone with a healthy moral force would reject that system, and refuse to cooperate especially after being victimized by it and seeing its corruption. They grow up terrorized, and then when they're trying to survive after being ostracized from their support network, these American heroes with shiny badges just become part of the monsters in their nightmare. They are just a different kind of monster, but even the most frightening of all because of the power they have over people, and they are stopping you from your attempts to survive, and being totally apathetic in it. I've even seen police officers laugh while they were terrorizing a victim of serious child abuse. This level of exposure will produce an army that will decimate your city which is certainly asking for it. Any city that is fine with terrorizing abused children, should probably be wiped from the face of the earth as a landmark termination to send the message. What does God have to do, to get the message across that he has created these needy ones?? He is their vindicator. Many of them are psychopaths because the exposure rate was left unchecked, to exceed what a person can tolerate. And so they will be the punishment to those who destroy the poor. But there are also so many homeless, who are precious and have such a rich spirit of good wholesome values. There are many precious needy ones that are part of me. Will always be. It's in that place of being at your lowest, that you find who's there in your need who cares. That is the greatest treasure a person could possibly find is real friends, who are all there in each other's need. That is heaven on earth, as it is in heaven. We must die for this cause to enter.

I found out later, that they pretty much were trying to scatter us all as far apart from each other as you could possibly get. 9-52 and Merlin with his dog Moomoo got some housing down by Mexico in such an aggressive barrio, they were mugged the very first day they were seen in the neighborhood by a gang of Mexicans. These two white guys from Oceanside stood out like Zebras in a herd of wildebeests. They even forced Merlin and 9-52 to take them to their apartment to see what they had in there they could steal, but they hadn't got anything yet. That was the end of their housing experience. They almost didn't survive it. They had to come back to Oceanside. At least here there was a chance of living. There were many stories like this that I was hearing from my group. A common theme was, two women had both had men who helped them survive over the years, and they both had dogs. Both of these women were expected to give up having their male protectors, and even their pet dogs they need for support. Somehow the housing is also included in this plan to sentence people to solitary confinement. It wasn't long before the whole crew was back in town. There were some of the old folks who got put in permanent housing, and also some of the handicap guests I had. My plan, which was the second stage to my model, could be used in our economic crisis as a win-win situation. My plan was to turn agricultural properties into trauma informed service sites- the shelter is where they learn to do their little part in farming. This could benefit farm owners who need farm hands, but can't afford the wages. This would be a barter for labor, but capitalism removes this ability.

All Lives Matter To Their Maker

data

Quantitative Research

i. Surveys- collect data from subjects who respond to a series of questions about behaviors and opinions, often in the form of a questionnaire.

1. Leading questions - (to a random stranger) how can a society have strong morals if everyone's forced to strive for self sufficiency?
2. Double barreled question- if everyone's financial problems are their own, who do they turn to when the sociopaths suck all the revenue out of the economy, and it all collapses?
3. Likert scale- rate of being offended 1 - 5 How often do you get upset when someone is being inconsiderate? Likert scale- rate of regret. 1 - 5. How much do you regret it when you don't consider someone else?

Interview- - Gloria Lynch, 87 years old. We talked in detail about the conscience being desensitized over the generations, and how people are so apathetic toward each other now, and how people aren't sensitive like they used to be, and are becoming self centered and materialistic, and how that's become the "norm." We both looked at each other with bewilderment (mouths open), and then she told me a little story of how life was in the 30's, in a little town on the other side of the river opposite of New York City named Coytesville New Jersey. There were seven streets, one traffic light, one post office, and one AMP Market. Gloria had a memorable Thanksgiving, when the preacher of the neighborhood church and other members brought a gigantic turkey dinner. After the amazing evening, and everyone was stuffed, Gloria's mother looked at everyone and thanked them all from the bottom of her heart, and said "you brought so much food, I don't know what to do with it all. Is there anyone in town short of turkey, and the preacher and other members confirmed, everyone in town had plenty of turkey." Glory leaned over to me with a big warm smile and said "everyone taking care of each other was the norm".

Front Psycol. 2018; 9: 614. Published online 2018 May 15. Doi: 10.3389/fpsyg.2018.0061

"In terms of evidence concerning aggravating factors, the potential role of mental health experts is primarily focused on only one issue: future dangerousness" [Edens, John F.; Cox, Jennifer. *Behavioral Sciences & the Law.* May/Jun2012, Vol. 30 Issue 3, p239-255].

4 PMCID:PMC5962766 PMID: 29867625 *Letter to the Editor Published: 19 December 2008 The neural correlates of moral decision-making in psychopathy A L Glenn, A Raine & R A Schug Molecular Psychiatry Volume 14, pages 5–6(2009)Cite this article*

Article metrics

- *2672 Accesses*
- *170 Citations*
- *11 Altmetric*
- *Metrics*
- *details*

Neuroimaging studies have used classic moral dilemmas to identify the neural circuitry underlying moral decision-making in healthy individuals, but it is unknown how this circuit functions in immoral, psychopathic individuals. In this functional magnetic resonance imaging (fMRI) study, we find that more psychopathic individuals show reduced activity in the amygdala during emotional moral decision-making, with particularly conning and manipulative individuals showing reduced activity in the entire moral neural circuit. These results provide initial evidence that psychopaths exhibit deficits in brain regions essential for moral judgment in normal individuals. Psychopathy is a personality disorder involving severe disruption in moral behavior accompanied by pronounced deficits in emotion. Emotion is argued to be a critical component of moral behavior.1 Highly emotional moral dilemmas have been found to evoke activity in the amygdala, medial prefrontal cortex, posterior cingulate and angular gyrus.1, 2 It has been hypothesized that persistent immoral behavior may result from deficiencies in some components of the moral neural circuit.3 We implemented a twice-replicated fMRI task involving classic moral dilemmas 1, 2 to examine the relationship between psychopathy and brain activity. We also examined whether four different factors of psychopathy (Figure 1, middle) were differentially related to neural activation during moral decision-making.

Negative association between psychopathy and brain activity during emotional moral decision-making. (Left) Higher total psychopathy scores (and all factors of psychopathy) were associated with reduced left amygdala activity (−21, −10, −14; 98 voxels, T=3.32, P=0.011, corrected). (Middle) Factors of psychopathy. (Right) The interpersonal factor was also associated with reduced activity in medial prefrontal cortex (−4, 60, 14; 98 voxels, T=2.67, P=0.030, corrected), posterior cingulate (0, −66, 35; 14 voxels, T=2.01, P=0.037, corrected), and angular gyrus (56, −66, 24; 56 voxels, T=2.50, P=0.012, corrected). No positive associations were significant. Anatomical labels: AMG, amygdala; PCC, posterior cingulate; MPFC, medial prefrontal cortex; ANG, angular gyrus. [Published: 19 December 2008 The neural correlates of moral decision-making in psychopathy [A L Glenn, A Raine, & R A Schug, Molecular Psychiatry volume 14, Pages 5–6(2009)Cite this article]

CONTENT PROVIDED BY

BrainFacts/SfN

Ventromedial prefrontal cortex

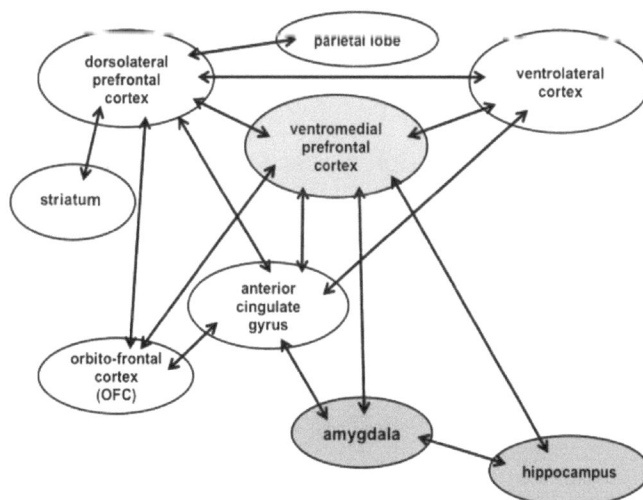

Different Contributions of the Human Amygdala and Ventromedial Prefrontal Cortex to Decision-Making

Antoine Bechara, Hanna Damasio, Antonio R. Damasio and Gregory P. Lee

Journal of Neuroscience 1 July 1999, 19 (13) 5473-5481; DOI: https://doi.org/10.1523/JNEUROSCI.19-13-05473.1999

"The somatic marker hypothesis proposes that decision-making is a process that depends on emotion. Studies have shown that damage of the ventromedial prefrontal (VMF) cortex precludes the ability to use somatic (emotional) signals that are necessary for guiding decisions in the advantageous direction. However, given the role of the amygdala in emotional processing, we asked whether amygdala damage also would interfere with decision-making. "

iii. Operational Definition- surveys: leading questions, double barrelled questions, and likert scales. New Testament scriptures are the approved remedy if applied.

iv. Correlations- Starchild's recovery from severe levels of psychosis without anti-psych meds correlates to my hypothesis about her cognitive breakdown being connected to her ability to come out of her psychosis. And because it was trauma related, she typically withdrew into isolation and escaping into the imagination. This left a great deficit of having almost no social construct of reality, and needed a trauma informed service site where the tenets of trauma informed care could be established through a peer approach; the first being safety and security." She found a healthy reality to fall into without needing meds. She had a place where Gorm wasn't around to get her vitals, and some care and conversation. She ate it up like candy. It was at the site she started having her awakenings that gradually progressed over time. She was simply having cognitive needs that were left unattended to. All programs that are deficit oriented were filled with inadvertent triggers that are part of the continual condition. This would lead her back into coping and escape mechanisms. Her immediate change in behavioral regularities after scolding her with love, put something in her that was of moral value. I do feel that her long stay in jail was part of me being able to catch her when her mind was clear, and not inebriated by some chemical. This correlates to the possible latent command to love by family of choice, in establishing moral force of conscience. She even once displayed what looked like shame on her face, which she seemed unable to have that capacity before. This needed a rescue from her plight, in which was in certain people stepping in to help. Those who are in her life. She's had people around her that do care, and were receptive to what I was saying about her condition and special needs. But she's left in a chaotic and violent environment with constant triggering, making it very difficult to water that seed of moral force that may have been planted in her. She did show signs after her awakenings that she wanted to be different, more her true self. But when she's triggered, that same old bad programming comes out. And she's constantly surrounded by things that would trigger her. Her stability is much in her boyfriend Gorm, (one of the checkers of the hood). He looks like a hard criminal, but he isn't really. He has a soft tender side, and has a solid reasonability to him. I've seen him admit he's wrong, when that is a miracle in these dark days. I don't think any of the world leaders could do that. When she is hurt emotionally, she screams out things that are of moral force; indignation at people being insensitive and victimization. Which- she is learning herself to be sensitive as her awareness comes more and more clearer. But she's like a six year old, with the emotional development of an infant, in need of much attention to help her develop. But it's no one else's problem. Why can't we put the play money into helping traumatized people? There's a toll bridge for this gross negligence. Cuz that's all that is really going on out here- just traumatized and neglected human beings in serious need of social development that would help them succeed. Problem is, her level of continual exposure is very severe. You have to know them, to know when they are showing progress so you can acknowledge and affirm it, and encourage them to the next step. Those are vital moments they need affirmations that they are growing and increasing. We miss these vital moments when we're not involved. I've been able to regularly acknowledge her progress, even though people still bitch about her behavior. What causes people to not see the good in others, is just them focusing on all the negative shit. We all have plenty of that. But her having someone to see these things, and affirm her in them has been a vital need in her progress. But then, the breaking up of the clan in the city moving us out, (clan as in whites, browns, and some very wonderful black members of the group), broke this connection. After not seeing Starchild for so long, I was glad to see that she was still pretty clear in her head, and coherent. Most of the homeless in that area were carrying on the cause, and I could see some of them healing each other by them just taking care of each other, and sharing their pain. It's what we're all supposed to be doing. This combination does create a reprocessing on a certain level. But much pain is still left unattended too. Pain that is so deep, you just hardly can go back to it for healing. Finding people that really care is what's needed.

v. primal data- The American Nightmare

Initial pathway- exposure: primal data of my experience in both functionalism, and conflict in my theoretical perspective. So both the construct, and destruct is relevant to determine influences in pathways. In my personal experience; I've suffered the illness of psychopathy, that has been severe levels of suffering in my soul- my primary pathway by exposure in which my spirit was revived by God's word taught by Yahshua's Apostles, which is his living spirit. HIs word saved me from going totally into the black.   The level of suffering I experienced in my soul is unexplainable. It is an experiential reality, not a gnostic one. My dad came back traumatized from the war, that only compounded a complex trauma from years of being beaten by his grandfather; an engineer from the ruff side of Oklahoma. Engineers from that circuit of railroad at the time were known to be among the most brutal of men. You had to be crazy to work on those old breaker cars because of the death rate.. I don't know all the details of his story, but I remember some bloody thanksgivings. He was the kind who would enjoy a good brawl. Bloody your nose, and give you a smile.

His friend Orris Eugene McGough married his daughter Joann. Orris (better known as grandpa Jimmy), became a world class prize fighter during the 40s- an Irish featherweight whose fighting name was *Tweek English*. He once fought the champ of France who broke his nose during the second round. Grandpa Jimmy's trainer used an old trick of spitting ice cold

rum in his face to bring him out of the shock. He came back to knock out the champ in the third round. Grandpa Jimmy served in wwii as a 101 airborne paratrooper. He was wounded when a bullet went through his right pectoral muscle, and ended his career as a prize fighter. Years later he did hard-time in prison when he struck a Cabi in New York for mouthing off to grandma Joann. The Cabi died after the fight, and so grandpa Jimmy went to prison for 6 years. During this time, grandma Joann was left to handle the children without grandpa. To make ends meet, she had turned to crime for survival.   Grandma got caught up in a liquor store robbery that got busted. She ended up the scapegoat cuz she was the getaway driver and was sentenced to 5 years in prison.

So because Jimmy and Joann were both in prison, my dad -Dale Aurthor McGough- ended up with his grandpa Virgil Wade. The family was disturbed by the levels of brutality inflicted on my dad during that time. This ended up a transference to me, a complexity of tyranny and being physically beaten on a regular basis. He started hitting me in the face when I was 7. My dad's exposure rate led him to becoming notorious for brutality. He was known to be the most feared man in that part of Downey at the time. He and all his friends became hard-core bikers. Suddenly his best friend Butch died of a gas explosion in an industrial accident. This sent dad into a whirlwind, and he shortly ended up in Viet-Nam right after. By the time he got back, he was a wreck; wild and out of control and prone to levels of extreme violence and on a very destructive path.

Dad's bike looked like this one, but was painted fuchsia red. The first time our living room became a blood bath was in 1974, when the biker party pad would get out of hand, dad would settle the matter real quick. It might have had something to do with squeaky stealing all the weed hanging in the garage. I just remember a big ventura speaker smashed into someone's head, and someone getting thrown through the sliding glass window. Sometimes the police would show up. The

next year in 1975 in a small cul de sac on colebrook, two police officers busted through the door when they saw Jim McDonald through the window. They totally destroyed our house chasing after him. I was run over in the wake of it. When they caught him, I watched them beat him nearly to death with their billy clubs. HIs nose was broken and his teeth were all over our floor. They would catch him not looking, and smash him right in the face with their clubs. I found out after they also broke his ribs. This was a very serious ptsd event for me. Dad later explained it was revenge- he was up for trial for putting an officer in the hospital. I immediately developed a sleeping disorder. I would regularly be up past 1 in the morning playing with my toys in the dark while everyone else was sleeping. My mom's friend Jolene who watched us caught on to this, and so started checking on me cuz she was up that late. Later they discovered I had a learning disability, that I later discovered had to do with the ADD and bipolarism you get from trauma and neglect. I had serious deficits. This ptsd event had been complicated by a threat I was experiencing by a bully named Brian. He would come around and terrorize us. Somehow after the traumatic event, I lashed out one day at him and hit him right in the face. A bunch of blood came out of his nose and he screamed and ran as I chased him. A couple winos yelled "get'm get'm". This would become a programmed response at being triggered by threats near home. A bully smasher started to come out. I didn't care who won the fight, I was aiming to rid the yard of danger. This grew as my life continued on this dangerous path. Dad had more parties that ended up in a brutal bloody beat down. They would shoot up in the bathroom. Mom knew when she smelled matches. I even witnessed my dad have a severe reaction during an overdose on pure cocaine. He was praying in the mirror, and turning in circles. Then he went into the living room, and started ramming himself headfirst into the wall. The paramedics came and had to bring him back to life with an adrenaline shot right into the heart. I started wandering the town by myself at this age. I would sometimes be gone all day. They once chased me down on my bike, threw me in the van, and drove me home. My parents tried to escape Downey and the whole crazy scene, and moved to Arizona. This led to a disruption in attachment with both parents at different points for me and my sister. Dad ended up back in Downey, and diving deeper into drugs. Mom started a new family in Arizona and repressed memories of the horror. My heart was torn to pieces and I was a wreck. This had effects on my sister, who was also devastated by our life. People were dying from speedballing. Danny ended up in prison for shooting a gay dude during a robbery. Jimmy and Joleen just drank their brains out. Roy lost his family, and while they were out on one of the bike runs, Roy stood up and said "I'm going for a swim", everyone laughed and said "what do you want us to tell your children"? Roy said, "tell 'm the river got me" and he jumped, blowing everyone's mind. The gentle giant died in the rapids. Harvey was a prankster, sometimes would jump out of the closet. One day he was found hanging from the tree with a rope around his neck and his head slumped over. Then he lifted his head and cackled. He had a harness under his shirt. One day he put his headset on with the 8-track playing Sergeant Peppers, stuck a 38 to his head, and pulled the trigger. That one was for real. Andy overdosed. Robert's family was part of the destruction. Steve brushed dad's front wheel and dad had to lay down the bike at 60 miles an hour; totally wiping out his mule, and bloodied him from head to toe. Right after that I had what would most certainly be the influence that would change the direction of my life. We watched a miniseries from the movie Jesus of Nazareth. There I saw for the first time, a representation of God's love in word and in deed. I didn't understand so much that these were actors, so it had a profound effect on me.

When I saw how he loved the needy, and gave himself for all, and how they just killed him, it reached the core of my being as a child growing up in a very scary and dangerous place. That Christmas, my other grandmother came to visit, grandma Charlotte. She noticed this new inspiration in me, and was intrigued by it and wondered where it came from. I told her about the movie, and she gave me my first Bible. She ended up being the one who watered the seed of my faith, And I simply grew in loving God's word, and wanting to be with him, who is love. Grandma Charlotte came from Winooski, Vermont. A tiny little town, with no real structure of government. Just friendly folk who all know and take care of each other. So she brought a certain command of moral obligation. She did this as she served. Her mother would feed the many with very wholesome home cooked food prepared with love. Often the Canadians would cross through the town, they called them canucks. My great grandma Mimi would invite them in, to get a warm bath, hot food, and clean clothes. Mimi was the spiritual strength in the family, and she was the one who kept the family together. Once she died , they went separate ways.

This heart to take care, and serve was passed on to me through her daughter, my grandma Charlotte Sprout. She was the representation that supported my new inspiration and helped me grow morally. This inspiration in God's word, was watered through a social development, a construction as Berger and Luckmann put it. Our emotional development is our moral decision making. She was very attentive, "how are you doing dear?" "Would you like me to make you something?" "Let me put some Bactine on that scrape". But we were able to develop a meaningful friendship over the years that went through many wonderful seasons, and also many storms. But in the end, we were very close.

The schools were not equipped to handle severe cases like mine. I was placed in a learning disability class in fourth grade. Many of the ruff kids were in there with the handicap. I ended up being drawn to what felt familiar to me, which was the kids who grew up in a similar environment as I did; smoking pot, drinking, fighting, and taking drugs. I graduated from L.D. class, but still had a hard time in the regular classroom. Or should I say the teachers had a hard time. I feel bad about how I was with some of them. They struggled to gain the children's attention from me. I was needing attention, but having to find the wrong kind of attention at the wrong place and time. I developed a clown form of attention-getting while growing up in a biker party pad. So now the teachers were left to be tormented by this unruly child with a clown spirit. My ninth grade history teacher asked me one day after class "could you do me a favor Rodney?, could you just not show up for class tomorrow?".

I think I was hurt and didn't understand. I even had one teacher grab me by the shirt, lift me off my feet and slam me on the desk. My girlfriend Rachel was trying to get me to get him in trouble for that. He saw me pinching her butt. I got sent to the office for a lot of swatts when I was young. Last grade finished was 9th. I was back with Dad in Downey, and going through the next stage of transference. During these years he would come home drunk on a regular basis. Physical beatings started to happen on a regular basis. It went on for so long on such a level, it took family intervention to rescue me from the situation. This intervention happened twice, where I had to be sent back to Arizona. The last time I ended up in an underground fight club. I was accustomed to violence and had an interest in Jeet-Kune-Do. I was the youngest in the group, but third in fighting rank. The one second in rank, was my trainer for a couple years. I discovered I had a threshold for violence when the brutality got to the point of sheer gore; biting and ripping faces, and huge bone breakers thirsty for blood. Once I saw the thirst for blood, it marked me in a way that changed my path. I started thinking about the movie Jesus, and I eventually became estranged from the ruff crowd as I returned to reading scripture.

The whole experience led me to being permanently expelled from an open campus school. In Arizona that is the last line for rejects too violent to be in the general population. Once they throw you out, it's all over. I was half way through 10th, so 9th grade was the last one finished. I started working under the table at car washes, and then found work doing all faze construction and demolition. Right after that, I ended up in a fist fight with my step dad John, that landed me homeless right after turning 17. This was a time of discovering the cold truth about the world. You can be starving in the face of squandering, and it's no one else's problem. Mom eventually gave me her old Chevy, but then traded me for a plane ticket because John couldn't sleep with me living in Arizona. So I ended up back in California, but this time I wasn't going to Downey. I went and stayed with Grandma for a year. I got to help her with the house and property, and I was able to get a job at the service station down at the bottom of the hill in Vista. I was trained to be a service station mechanic, to take care of Miss Jones like she was my own grandma. As shops became more corporate, less private, antisocial norms were handed down for me to adapt to. Now it was; sell the work and parts, even if Miss Jones doesn't need it right now. I was applying for a job at a shell station, and the owner said "I don't hire mechanics to save customers money." Suddenly, what I was originally taught was good work, was now bad. I was appalled by the notion, and walked out of the interview. But I was soon faced with the reality that this appalling notion was becoming a norm in the industry. While working at Chevron, my boss wrongfully charged an old lady 1,200 dollars for the mechanics' incompetence to diagnose the problem. Missing really badly, I asked," what was the code?" Walter said "faulty distributor reading." I noticed the oil around the valve cover and I asked "did you check the timing belt, it might have slipped?". Walter; "you don't know what you're talking about. You ain't no tech." So I watched in agony as he kept replacing relays, and electronic components. He even replaced a 900 dollar computer that couldn't be returned when it came out that wasn't the problem. You'll never guess what it turned out to be- a freakin timing belt. Job total $1, 295. Timing belt job $95.

I didn't give the old man too much shit, cuz I knew he couldn't handle it. The customer Veronica, an elderly retired violinist, came crying to me because she was suddenly in a financial crisis, and felt like she was robbed. I felt responsible because we had a little friendship, but I was ashamed I didn't tell her what really happened because I didn't want to lose my job. That's when I started doing side jobs for a friend who owned a shop. Conscience couldn't remain working for monsters. I became isolated over the years, and diving deeper into scripture that included the prophecies of the end times. I also became a student of sociology, starting with the works of Erich Fromm. But this was part of my habit of taking textbooks into my hiding place, but not learning their disciplines, or be constrained by their academic standards. So my imagination was filled with scriptures, of how it was back then in the times of Jesus' flight, and glory, and those united in his blood. But this remained only in my thoughts, because I wasn't able to find any churches that actually believe what the scriptures say that disciples are supposed to do. I refused to give up what was written. I made a pact with God, to never let someone tell me the scriptures mean something other than what is simply written. I could see as a young boy how the Apostles were clearly giving God's commands, and people were deceiving themselves that they didn't mean what they wrote. That they somehow said one thing, but really meant some other thing; as if they are some kind of tricksters or something. This led me to not having an adequate representation to follow, and was simply left to find it myself in scriptures. As I dove deeper into the word, I found myself more and more withdrawn from the world. I wasn't finding the fellowship depicted in Acts, where they lived together and had all things in common. Any attempt to share these things, resulted in me seeing more and more how people just generally didn't believe the word of God. Even preachers of any church. I eventually found a wife, and had a son named Jeremiah, but I always called him bubba. It was at this time that the spiritual harvest of my faith of learning from the New Testament scriptures was in the compassion I found myself having for homeless teens and children who suffered the conditions that I experienced, but ended up in an orphanage, or foster care facility. I found a link through that work that made me eligible for work as a councilor because of my personal experience, and survival of it. It started at a foster care facility where I was trained and tested to be a State Certified Counselor.   So I went through the necessary requirements, and got my certification. Immediately though, I became disturbed by the way the children were being treated. They started with training me in restraint, and gaining physical control of the children. These techniques seemed very harsh, and insensitive to them. I felt very uncomfortable with the restraint techniques. It was triggering me emotionally, and I didn't fully understand them back then. I became critical of these techniques, and even had people removed from position because of using excessive force and traumatizing the children. I could see right away this cycle of children not doing what they were supposed to do, and then going through a process of forced restraint. But it always seemed unnecessary, and cruel. Here the children aren't getting the direction with a will that would put some worth in them, and give them something to do with their energy. And then are forced to just sit there in a chair, and restrain their energy to do something. Then when they would get restless, and doing things, they would get tackled by some big galute and restrained by leg scissoring. Then transfer of molestation would happen when councilors would take a break from them, and go in the backyard and talk or something, and an older 12 year old would take advantage of a younger 6 year old. Usually the ones who suffered severe levels of neglect, and had essentially no cognitive development were the victims of these events. The counselors would come down on the children with this real heavy criminalization of their behavior, but I felt it was the counselors who needed the scolding. I started to try and take control of this helter-skelter by simply getting involved with them, and getting to know them on a personal level to try and reach their broken heart to mend it. Those who suffered severe neglect were usually left in a room alone all day, as probably how they were left with their natural parents. One named Cris had no moral development, he would jab a stick into the eye of another child without understanding the severity of his actions. I tried to deal with this by getting him to understand what he was doing. He seemed to lack understanding even of what I was saying. It was discovered though that I had some kind of grace with the children, getting them all together, and keeping them in order and teaching them as they learn to participate together, in music and projects. This made them very excited to be apart, and they were showing an increase in their behavior. This began to expose the clinical techniques as being ineffective. I was brought into a meeting about how I was with the children, after I had them make instruments by putting pebbles in boxes, and having small sticks to beat on boxes to make drum sounds, while I played the children's guitar that I finally got tuned up.

We were having a blast jamming out in the living room. They were all behaving very well, and they were getting so much of the kind of attention they were needing. I had them in the palm of my hand. I could command them, and they were faithful to obey because I was their friend. I was told in the meeting that I was being fired from the job because my methods were seen to be childish, and not having the right authority over them. That was a very difficult moment, children were crying that I was having to leave, and I was quite emotional myself. One guy who saw what was going on, let me in on the plan they had to build padded rooms in the garage to lock the children in when they are out of line. He decided he couldn't handle working there any more, and I decided I couldn't handle it either.

Right away, I began working in Oceanside around 1999, with a nonprofit called Stand Up For Kids. It was the #1 nonprofit at the time. I was able to come right in, and handle things. The first house was rented on mission after doing homeless outreach for a year on the streets, handing out food bags and hygiene kits. When the house was opened, all these mothers who were there did not know how to handle the kids, and it was becoming a disaster area. Every night when they were kicked out at 10:00 PM, the house would be a complete disaster area. It took the woman and I till midnight to clean it up. They came to me to try and help them. So I said, "if you want me to help, I need money to deadbolt that pantry door, and I need to see a signature that they have completed their clean up chore. So the women got me the money and a printed list of all chores, and a box for a signature. The first night, everyone enjoyed their stay, and were faithful to do their chores. Just before closing, the runt completed the final chore of scrubbing the toilet and bathroom floor. The house looked beautiful. I was so proud of them and they did such a good job, and the women had more time to just be there emotionally for the kids, which is the most important of all. This became the established way even after I had left. It was difficult for me to be a "Stand Up For Kids" counselor for homeless teens and children. Some of the most detrimental experiences they suffered were with police officers who terrorized them by vagrancy laws. One of the boys had serious bruising from handcuffs, and burn marks from a cigarette that he said an officer put out on his arm, because he threw the cigarette on the ground lit when the officer told him to put it out. This drew me to the end of my threshold of tolerance. It was triggering me emotionally, and it was very intense. I have a rage when it comes to levels of severity, and a bully smasher comes out. I knew I was in danger of getting in trouble because of this level of severity. The purpose of the organization was to find ways to help the homeless children and teens because the bureaucratic laws deemed them a liability, so they couldn't get assistance at homeless service settings with food, clothing, hygiene, or shelter.

This left them unprotected and at the mercy of predators who lurk the streets looking for the vulnerable. The youngest I counseled was 11 years old who made a living selling sex toys on the beach. And the rational mind has found all these valid reasons to protect everyone in the stratas of society from being liable for these poor helpless human beings bearing the weight of their oppression. And I have to say as someone who's been getting involved with these abandoned youth, after they find their mechanisms of escape from their nightmare, nothing drives the needle deeper than substance control and vagrancy laws that criminalize them for their afflictions. And condescension from those who are so above them in their fantasies. Be warned all who are under oath to serve with authority, *those who oppress the poor are in contempt of their maker*" Proverbs 14:31. But no matter the examples that we have, the point isn't the rationality, the point is the value. Wrong values break hearts. What is important to us? Later on, I eventually became like a shrew, holding a standard to the staff about boundaries which led me to having meetings with a very wonderful lady who was the project manager, who had a very good way with me. She was my first real teacher in Trauma Informed Services.   It all came down to them needing people to go deeper and really be a friend and brother to them. But this was a boundary the organization wasn't willing to cross. But I could tell, they weren't really getting what they needed.   The gospel of my faith said, they needed a family. I really felt the need to move on, and was greatly saddened, but had hopes my heart could be fulfilled.

I really started to focus on my son Jeremiah. He was our only son, and we were quite an amazing family for a while. We have a lot of memories of me teaching him how to ride his bike, and ride his skateboard. I was watching him during the day while his mother worked at the office, and doing mechanic work at my friend's shop in Vista. Clarkes Automotive. Ron was owner and general tech, and his brother Rich was co-owner and machinist. He had some Bridgeport equipment; mills, plains, and lathe. I was hardline- engine, driveline, and chassis. I was also a carburetor specialist, and had a carb work bench in the shop. These were guys I hung out with since the mid 80s. It was a car club. We all had our hot rods, and worked in the auto repair industry. Sometimes I would have my son come to the shop, and strip the bolts out of an engine on the floor or something. I got him some Dickies, and a little tool box. I spent a lot of time with my son, filling his mind as much as I could. Probably more than he could handle. DogTown and Z Boys documentary came out, and me and my friend Big Daddy got restoked. So we busted out some skaters and hit the hills. I went back to doing *Bert*, and working on my power slides. After several years, we had a Thomas Guide full of downhill courses we mapped out with our pins where we would bomb and carve hills going from one street and spilling into another. The longest one was a 2 mile ride starting from the top of a mountain on a wide smooth black-top road with sloping turns and big black waves. We would leave one car at the bottom, and drive up to the top, and jump out and skate all the way down. I soon learned the danger of bombing hills, You never really plan on going 60 mph. It gradually gets to that point by misjudging the down slope. You have to be able to powerslide at high speed to keep from reaching stupid levels of deadliness. My son became a part of our skating sessions. It was some of our most memorable moments. Our favorite spots were where the big industrial parks were in the hills, with lots of smooth transitions with big swooping slopes that shot you like a big black wave into a tunnel of oleanders that you had to squat all the way down to make it all the way to the end with a hard front slide to avoid the cement planter. But on the streets, you have to be on constant lookout. Big Daddy saved me a number of times. Once I heard his whistle, looked to the left, and saw I was dropping into the path of an 18 wheeler going about 45. AAA!!!! That high speed drop-n-slide had to be programmed. Thankfully it was. I was realizing I was leading my son into some dangerous stuff. And then he was starting to do some dangerous stuff. That's when I started losing interest in the stupid levels of deadliness. It's very easy to slip into, and it's so gradual you don't realize what you're doing, or how you are influencing other people who look up to you.

I decided to move away from mechanics and help my wife with her work, and we eventually had a business of our own. I just would write out a presentation for a company after learning their production history, and Tricia would do the graphics in the old word rap system of code entry. So for six thousand dollars, we would do web brochures, data entry, and Tricia would set up their email and set up booths at trade shows. This was at the beginning of web advertisement. So we exploded and made up to 80 thousand in the fifth year. We tried to get out of the renting world, because it was such a waste, and we weren't having anything to show for it. But prices were horrible, and we ended up in a high risk loan on a 324,000 dollar condo in Oceanside. Only six months later, we found out it wasn't even habitable. They hid the fact that the entire sewer system was destroyed by the pine tree roots. We were totally robbed, and we had to forfeit everything. The stress was too much for us. We ended up getting a divorce that year. But my wife said something as to having believing I was suppose to fulfill what God put in my heart for tending to the orphans and widows on the streets, and going through the discipline written in scriptures, of learning to be content with the cloths on our back, and the food provided

112

by the work set before you in serving the needy. This would include even going without shoes and walking on the hard ground, and finding contentment there for the purpose of serving the needy.   So I just gave up my half of the house, car, and business so Tricia would have enough to take care of our son. Plus, she was the one who really made the business what it was, and made it all happen by being on that cutting edge.   It was a devastating time for us. We were all traumatized severely. I ended up on the streets of Oceanside, and Tricia ended up taking my son and moving to Texas. This devastated my family. Again, I found myself totally alone.

The police in Oceanside that did the homeless beat were ruthless.   I began the testing I felt I was supposed to go through for some reason.   I ended up at a soup kitchen where people would gather for dinner. I wasn't the type to have a camp, but would just find a small spot to sleep, and leave at dawn. I met a woman at the time, who knew a community in Vista that believed in giving up your life. So I began going to their gatherings, and eventually moved in. Although at first, I didn't stay very long. I had to ease into the cultural shock.   But I would just keep popping up at the Foothill house. I ended up falling into a rebound situation with the woman I met. We both had just had our families broken up, and so we both had voids that needed to be filled emotionally. She had children that I began to focus on their needs, which were pressing. She also was left in a desperate situation, and needing a lot of help with even the house work. I stayed a few months with her in her garage, but then became her boyfriend until her mother used this situation with her having a strange homeless man around, to call CPS and take her children away. I learned that this had been going on since her first born was a toddler who was now 12.   So I ended up back on the streets, but helping her on the side with paralegal work to try and get her children back. She was in a constant state of emotional turmoil over the detention of her children.   And I felt bad that they were doing this to her, and the fact I made it look bad on her because I was a homeless man that just moved in.   Much to my surprise though, I was able to find inconsistencies in the social workers initial detention report. I sent her lawyer my findings, in which she used to cross examine the social worker in court- who then took the 5th when she was unable to respond to the questions about the inconsistencies that were used to substantiate detaining the children.   The problem was, social workers are 5th wavers; they are all required by law to be completely forthcoming in their reporting. So she was removed from the case, and another worker was assigned. This is where the children should have been returned to their mother because the detention was found to be illegal. So the judge now has God to face for his judgment and the truth will be known.

As far as I could see, the mother took care of them for the most part. She was a certified LVN, and was well educated in medical procedures. She would read to them every night before bed, and had good routines with bathing. She always kept them fed, and had many moments of time with them during the day, though she was a little like a kid herself. But she did have healthy expectations of her children, and would deal with them the best she knew how. The point was, the children did know she loved them. We were both damaged, and in the ruff. We weren't Sunday goin model Americans. We came from a place of people speaking with foul mouths, and were subject to inappropriate behavior. We would yell and cuss people out for their bullshit. We smoked pot, and listened to rowdy music. That was about it. But we did try to be good people on the inside, and to know God's word and do what we were supposed to do. We generally just didn't understand these emotional instabilities we had.   The grandmother was demonizing the mother in front of the children as if she didn't love them, when the mother was a victim of child abuse. She was demonizing the very child she abused, and then took her children away from her instead of just helping her. As far as I could tell, her mother had no sign of conscience.   She even seemed to be latent in preadolescence- and in a hyper-rational state of living in a fairytale land. Her strife against her daughter over the children, was a demonstration of how infantile her mind was. It was like a high school nemesis who has seething hatred for the prom queen. She was the type to be obsessed with her little girl much like the ones who have professional models for children. They can become brutal dictators and abusive to their subjects of this obsession. When her daughter rebelled and rejected this after so long, the mother attacked her physically, then began to focus on her daughter's children. I could tell by having an insider view, that the system was a part of this woman's mental illness, and CPS was giving the children to someone who was not psychologically competent to care for the children. By the government getting involved in these domestic affairs, which I don't even know if they have jurisdiction, they traumatized the children severely by disrupting their attachment to their mother simply by going on hear-say, and then siding with the grandmother in this tug war; harming them psychologically by participating in alienating the children from their mother.   The impact on the children and mother was devastating. Though I was sleeping out on the beaches of Oceanside, I still continued to study the CPS status reports and I found more inconsistencies. I again sent my paralegal work to her lawyer, in which she again used to cross examine the social worker who, like the first one, was unable to answer the questions of the inconsistencies in her reports, that were making the mother out to not be cooperating when she was. She was also removed from the case. I know the mother was cooperating, because she showed me how she had made all her appointments even though they were almost impossible to make given her situation in financial need, and not having dependable transportation. It was like they used her financial plight as a reason to deny reunification with her children. This was a shocking reality, that you don't have parental rights if you find yourself in financial crisis. I ran into a very special man who also did paralegal work for these types of cases, who was also homeless because he suffered from having a neurological disorder that greatly impaired his motor skills. But he was very intelligent, and brought social workers to justice by a law that was passed that found CPS workers to be using their position of power to extort money. The workers would get 27, 000 dollars for each child that was adopted out if the parent was found to be harmful to them somehow. There is a cross cultural and cross millennial documentation of this form of extortion in the book of Job. The orphan was snatched from the bosom of the poor widow to pay off a debt- [Job 24:9]. This is where I started to see what was going on when the new worker replaced those removed from the case. They were just as ruthless as the ones before them. They all seem to just jump on to this bandwagon of grandma demonizing her daughter, while alienating the children from their mother. After doing everything they told her she had to do to get her children back, they refused to reunite them and just adopted them out to the grandma anyway without substantive due cause. We were terrorized by these forces, who hold nothing sacred. I was sorry and frustrated from all the hard work ending up in defeat. The several months I was with her, she did end up pregnant and having a boy we named Zephyr. I quickly realized we fell into the typical rebound when people lose their families. I wasn't able to be there for him, but would help in ways I could on the outside. I would even go shopping for her and bring her milk if she needed it. She could just call me if there were needs. Our attempts at being partners, just resulted in us hurting each other. We decided to go separately to the twelve tribes community, and give up our lives there.

The only subjects I completed in Jr college was engine rebuilding and machining, and fuel systems and carburetion. And also classical guitar, music theory, and composition. But again with the music, it was mostly isolated learning from textbooks. The engine and carb shops were different. They created an environment in the shop that I was used to, and many in there were also in the ruff socially. When I was forming my hypothesis and signing up for classes at Mira Costa, I was signed as a disabled student with special needs. I didn't know if I could do it, because I never learned to fit into public school. And I knew it would trigger old wounds. I was going to all my classes on time, and being up with the lessons. But I was struggling because it seemed like the professor wasn't teaching sociology. Even students came to me, saying "I feel she's not even teaching us." When it came to social conflict, she would not bring in any of the pillars of sociology into the conversation. And then leaving it to uneducated students to use their discernments on solutions. So I would start to try and bring these socially educated experts of sociology into the conversation, which only resulted in an interruption. I mentioned this to the disabled students office, who didn't know what to say. I even had students come to me, saying they were ready to march into battle. Some of the youth were looking to me to start a countercultural movement the way the sociology professors used to do. But I didn't know how to do that. After a few weeks, I was growing tired of the whole facade going on in the classroom. The professor never learned about the law of contraction that was vital to the conversation about family in this society, and then after I brought it up a few times, she still refused to teach sociology. It was like the twilight zone. It was exactly what Marcuse said in his book One Dimensional Man, 'the rational mind would get to the point of removing all critical thought and standard from society, so that it only becomes an interruption'. And that is exactly what was going on in the sociology classroom. The critical thought and standard of the pillars of sociology, was removed even from the sociology classroom, so that it only was an interruption. I was finally asked to leave for interrupting the class, and I simply said "I don't know what you call this, but it isn't sociology." I told the students, "if you want to learn about sociology, read One Dimensional Man by Herbert Marcuse." And then I walked out. I did want to continue with my social psychology professor though, cuz she's really cool. And she's totally with it on the C.E.B.T. She was ready to make the streets of Oceanside a learning service site, but I was struggling and hurt by what happened. I had to drop my classes. But I went on with my research, because I could tell the whole system in the university when it comes to research, creates by its regulation a sabotage in which nothing can really be determined. A true learning service site has to be raw, and in the base reality through participant observation in the actual environment undisturbed to run its natural course. The observer has to have the eyes of experience in his observation. You have to have been there, and experienced the dynamics involved in which to find that spurious correlation that reveals the causation. Bureaucracy is all about protecting special interests, which are not willing to make those sacrifices to find this pertinent information. It is even against their interest to have these things determined. They aren't so much caring about making these determinations, because they're not so much affected until it all comes crashing down like the twin towers. Then when people are running and screaming, and jumping off towers do they finally realize the seriousness of the situation.

Unfettered acquisition will create the most cruel and evil society that is doomed to utter destruction in the most brutal and vicious way. The most wicked principal man could ever have in his ethical programming, is the principal of a market in which sociopaths are free to acquire the entire economy, with all its land and resources, and then tell everyone "we don't have to serve you." It is the ethic of 'want comes first' that creates those kinds of societies. I was shocked to hear Tucker Carlson of Fox News raging about "bums" being set up in nice places to live off the streets. His anger comes from this ethic that also includes an indignation when people that don't have money are not suffering because they're not working. He really wants the common worker to have the carrot to strive for while he's turning the millstone, usually never really getting it after all the turning. The entire nation was spit in the face, and told "fuck you." by its leaders. And now everyone is supposed to just get their ass to work? By what morale do they carry on in this sham? There was a betrayal that has consequences that are sure to come. He's oblivious to this because of his achievement in the stratification. He's also oblivious to the morale a man needs to keep him working. The contract that replaced the patriarchy was burned. The edict of peace went up in flames, as millions of peoples with millions of hours of investment went down the tubes as their lives were destroyed. This was adjacent to giant corporations' further achieving public dependency on CEOs. So in his rational fantasy, Tucker Carlson thinks helping the needy is the problem with getting people back to work. This passing the blame on those at the bottom, is part of dodging the reality of where the blame is. That kind of mind doesn't understand the concept of broken hearts. He thinks families should just be able to be destroyed, and people just move on and get their asses to work and stop whining about their destroyed family and children. God's gonna save us from the lunatics. After your soldiers have lost their morale to carry on the battle, you need to look at the premise of what that morale was based on. The system and its leaders have failed the people miserably. The good police have been resigning because it's gone too far, and leaving us at the mercy of xbox heroes with badges programmed to shoot the bad guy, even if it's a 90 year old granny. They have had the police abandon their oath to "serve and protect." And now are the modern crackers, and they're crackin' ya on the slave drive. And if your broken heart makes you unable to cope in society, you should just go die a slow death on the streets of hellville.

During the time I was running my camp, I was helping on the team at Humanity Showers, with Jordan Verdin. He was a big part of spreading my message. He was a big contributor to Camp On Wheels. I began to see these canopies of different specialists show up. One was a chiropractor, the other a barber, and a free store for clothing. One of the canopies was for

McAllister- a drug rehab organization. I started probing them to see if they were trauma informed. I first asked if they were, and the main person running the nearby clinic said "yes, we're trauma informed." I began to ask other questions to try and determine as to the level of being informed. Some of the responses were quite the opposite of what you would expect from Trauma Informed Care. They still appeared to be deficit oriented, and coordinated with law enforcement in the criminalization of those that research has determined to be trauma survivors. This was exposed when they were put on the voucher project for my camp. There were several cases of just throwing them right back out in the street because they approached it by criminalizing them, rather than using an empathy strengths based approach. These were people that were showing corrective emotional responses by my approach that was a peer approach after establishing safety and security. I was not allowed to handle the situations with any of them. It was solitary confinement, which is an obvious set up for failure. Dystopia.

Right behind the motel, was another small row of tents that were being forced to move out, and bulldozers laying the same rocks they dumped on my site. One of the watchmen from my camp called me to tell me of a lady who was left by the Hot Team. They did the vouchers for those in the tents, and then had a truck come by and throw away all the tents and bedding. One of them was a lady in a wheelchair, that they just left there after she was reacting because of the way they were handling her. So they just left her there with no tent or bedding, and never came back. Hot team would not respond to me. It was obvious they abandoned post, and left her out there. I was spurred to get back to my storage, and find something for her. I did find something small but substantial for her. I could tell she was simply a severe case of trauma. Her verbal outburst almost seems to be a tourette syndrome type of seizure that happens in the left temporal lobe. I haven't worked with the syndrome, so I'm only familiar with case studies. But I noticed that those who have # 4 temporal lobe ADD symptoms that, according to Amen includes probability of head trauma, experience what looks like a petit mal seizure when they are triggered to relive the trauma. The result is profane verbal impulse. This is the number one reason she is denied services on all levels- food, shelter, resources, right to live in general. Also, she's crippled from a collapsed spine, and a serious leg injury. She eventually ended up over on the other side of town near the place I had rented a small music studio space near the soup kitchen, where I could do my peer support. I was continually making the effort of keeping her alive, while she was left at the mercy of the dangers on the street, with no one who would take her in. One night she was the victim of a hate crime, where a large man and his girlfriend ran up and grabbed her tent, and started tearing it up while she was in it. I ran up and said "what are you doing? I bought her that tent. That is her tent." I first thought they were accusing her of stealing their tent. But I quickly realized, it was a hate crime and they were using force to remove her from the neighborhood. I was not able to stand and watch it. I stopped it, and was attacked by the man. When I realized he was drunk, and didn't really know how to fight, I just held my ground to defend her. They eventually went away. Police were soon there, telling her she had to move. I had spent a whole day helping her move to a spot not blocking the sidewalk. But she was immediately ticketed for illegal camping. All programs refuse to help her -even vouchers for motels- and the only thing they know how to do is criminalize her and keep ticketing her while denying her services. Even the soup kitchen refused to give her a shower, because she took too long to get out, and she spoke "using inappropriate language." Right after she was forced to take down her tent, it rained and even hailed on a day it was expected to get down to 30 degrees that night. So I went to the soup kitchen, and told them about the crisis and how she was in danger of dying from hypothermia because she was wet, and all her bedding was soaked, and it was going to be freezing that night. After spending 90 minutes getting her up to the resource center of the soup kitchen, they denied her services because of the inappropriate language that was offensive to the staff. She was left to die of hypothermia because of her offensive language that only comes out during one of her episodes. A sign of tourettes, is that the episode doesn't reflect behavior regularities. She normally doesn't use profanity when speaking. It's not part of her 'character' or personality. I went to McAlister right next door, and told them about the risk of her dying, and to communicate with the Hot Team in which they did. None of these programs responded to someone traumatized and in danger of hypothermia. Here, research has determined these people to need trauma-informed care, which was removed as an option by the city forcing us out and destroying my peer support, and then leaving these people to just be continually traumatized and then dehumanize them when they are triggered. This is a retaliation for vicarious trauma, that causes further trauma to the afflicted by criminalizing them while they are reliving traumatic events. This is how it becomes worse for those out there. Here in California, they try to combine the 'trauma informed care', with the criminalization process which is the most ridiculous thing I've ever heard of in my life. Trauma informed care, is opposite of all the deficit oriented approaches that research has proven to make them worse. But they don't care. The reason you cannot have any of these churches, police, or even these clinical white coats addressing the problem, is because they're all 'above' homelessness. All hope lies in tenet # 2, peer support to get to # 3, trust and transparency, where healing begins. Someone who's been there, that they know and feel comfortable with. The system actually keeps them from this support, and forces them to go to torture chambers. It is proven in the field of psychotherapy, that they must achieve the fifth tenant which is control and empowerment. You ruin this if you start off by taking control of them.   This is also proven to cause them to relive terror. The churches condescend on their wounds with principals, and communicate to them that they are in that situation because they don't have it right with Jesus. By this, they tell abused children it was all their fault. I've even explained how this destroys the souls of abused children, and these christian heroes just don't care! According to the DSM, they are probably sociopaths. If you don't care about hurting them, you are a sociopath and should stay away. Get it? Get a real job, and leave these needy ones to be cared for by those who value their life.   Those of us who care about them, have absolutely no say-so in how things are conducted.   There is a phenomena related to the condition of sociopathy in capitalistic society, that apathy rules and has all the say-so. Apathy has been proven to trigger those who suffer from ptsd, and demands to be the one to deal with these victims.   The more apathy, the more say-so. The more empathy -what they need for healing to start- the less say-so. All the homeless need protection from those who continually hurt them psychologically.   Out of all this, what really keeps them from really getting anything they need, is the plight of them needing a residence with an address to get anything. No place to receive mail where you live stops it all. This is why there essentially isn't homelessness in Finland, because they have this simple understanding that typical Americans just can't get.   It is the 'house first' economy, because they are in reality and understand you need a residence to be able to adequately function as an employee. A child could understand that for God's sake. Police push you into gutters and outskirts where you can't easily be able to be out there and able to work.   No place to take a shower, and have clean clothes, and you just walk in there with leaves in your hair and dirt on your face??   What the hell are you talking about?   The lady in the wheelchair has a collapsed spine from a crippling condition that she already has disability insurance and ssi, but she's not able to receive it because of no mailing address.   This is one of the number one problems, that the usual Brother Benno's mail service would just not be anywhere they could stay, and so end up miles away. Without a residence, you cannot legally expect them to go get work.   That is pushing them to perjure themselves on their applications that warn with the threat of felony charges. You can't be expected to do anything without an address according to the unwritten rule of survivability in this society. You can't get an id, a bank card, a job, a place to live, or anything legally.   That is grand entrapment.   So many wish they could work. I could have been having

them work. The fact that this structured government could allow all these requirements to

survive pile up and not be provided while criminalizing them for it, means they should all be

arrested and thrown into jail.   Another thing that is probably the number one hold up when it

comes to all these ptsd cases that make up the chronic homeless and drug abuse problem, is

that emotional trauma means loud screaming and yelling in moments when you are triggered.

This emotional instability is really what makes it so there is nowhere to go to live or work.   This

was one of the major points in the second part of my model, of having them getting their therapy

on farms out in the open away from the general public. The first key to my model is peer

support. All psychotherapy is a peer approach. For us peers, this yelling and screaming isn't

so much a big deal. Sometimes it can even feel like home which can become a pleasant

memory after reprocessing.   This loud factor of trauma is the old ladies' problem of really being

able to be in a shelter, or program, or share a house. One episode ruins it all over again. That's

what it narrowed down to with the Hot Team leaving her after throwing all her bedding away.

She was there loading up in the van when she got triggered, and then the loud reaction made it

so they told her she wasn't going to be able to go.   Horrible. Here I would have been able to

have a place for these serious cases, but the big money in control just wanted to smash Rodney

and his friends, and kick 'em down the road. Slime balls will not allow any solution to the hell

that is going on right now. Is anyone getting it?? It is all going to burn any minute now. Are you

getting it???   They are really closing them off from being citizens of the United States of

America, and leaving them in a state of needing refuge, while still having the little plaque on the

Statue of Liberty. Now they welcome the money, while veterans become poor American

refugees. America is dead. It was killed by slimeballism. Those of us who care want to find

places to help them get the real help they need, so they're not just dumped on the streets and

storefronts.   But the government does not allow it. They are the ones who choose to have it

that way, but brainwash people to think the poor and homeless choose to live in squalor and be

terrorized on the streets.   The system failed the kids, and they don't want to own up to it.

Politicians don't own up to shit, and don't have to unless someone makes them.   So do you

think that you can deny the masses a social system to help because of your ideology, and think

they won't flood your cities?   I've watched the 6 point cycle of how these programs make

money on the homeless for years. Millions of dollars come for the problem, vouchers are

issued, case management provided, something was wrong with your urine, they toss you back

out in the streets, and start all over again.   People get paid, while the homeless stay homeless as their hope dwindles away. To the orgs and institutions, nothing is broken. They get paid, and go home and have a wonderful life. Solving homelessness is not even their goal, or their problem. They have no incentive. Keeping the homeless homeless is even job security. No homeless, no job. It's a business that makes lots of money with a CEO. This is why no solution could ever come about as long as CEO's just make everything into a corporation. The whole country is a corporation. Even families now are corporations. It's the sickness ruling society with no check or balance. I was disgusted to find out that, out of all the efforts of people trying to build small tiny home villages for them to live, nothing was able to come about because of bureaucrats who had all these rules to stop us. But somehow, there was a tiny home village for those not homeless. Isn't that interesting? So it was ok for people just wanting to be relieved from pressures of the cost of living in San Diego, but not for people trying to help the homeless. Why? One answer- slimeballs ruling. What's going to devastate the world with nuclear war? Slimeballs ruling. I was thankful for the governor turning away from the police option, to just housing them. But it is inhumane if people who are crippled and can't work are left in solitary confinement with no community. Their sanity also has to be on the bill. The spin on racism is to cover up that slimeballs come in all sorts of colors and shapes, and they are the enemies at the top exploiting good citizens at the bottom who also come in all sorts of colors and shapes. So racism is a spin to cover up that slimeballs are the enemy of all races. A sign that fascist dictators are taking over, is when they started acting like Nazi's. Hitler had a way of dealing with those hc thought were "life not worthy of life." His was probably more merciful than the years of torture these ones were assigned to. That is what these programs are determining, and it generally is only if you can make money. If you are disabled, you are considered in this system of whitewashed christians, 'life not worthy of life.'

iv. Correlations- Fantasy phenomena: People are acting like no one knows why all these people are dumping into the streets after the 1% decided to not redistribute the wealth and resources to the 99%. It's a phenomenon to see these people wondering why. It's simple math. 5th grade I think. A republic cannot function with the structure depending on only 1%. Everyone needs to understand that simple math. How can you even talk about the free market anymore? Free to what? Who? This seems that these ideas can only be entertained by the hyper-rational mind. Every economy has a threshold of how many heads it can support. Just a few heads can take all of it so it won't support anyone else but them. They set up a scam that just keeps taking and compromising, even in national crises. They are even exploiting the crisis. Even when everyone is going to fall through the cracks but the 1%, the machine can't stop sucking their blood until they're bone-dry, and left on a curb with a little piece of cardboard. When the nation had moral fiber, slow torturous death was worse than a bullet in the head. They've gone to the point of assigning everyone to slow torturous death while they play with their toys. That is the mind at the helm right now. There is nothing to talk to them about. They are only fit to be chained and caged. Their liberalism robs our right to live, and actually destroys vitality and solitary. They are a menace to all mankind, and threaten his very existence.

Correlation to support cause of homelessness, drug abuse, and the emotional factor- the Eagles broke up, and Joe Walsh was ruined emotionally. This is a sign that his heart was deeply in the band, and then was broken. If you see what happened to him the following years, he was a broken man. It was amazing to see him come back the way he did. I was so surprised to see him talking in a sober manner about the situation. Disbanding breaks the heart of those who have their heart in the band. If there is no broken heart, their heart wasn't in the band, but just in it for themselves while keeping their heart reserved elsewhere. Some just might not have a heart. We can make it all about our own dreams, while not in it for the dreams of those serving in our dream. If everyone is serving their own dream, how is it that the dreams of others aren't crushed in the effort? And how are we going to maintain our conscience in the wreckage we overlook, as we move on? The heart of the band is the moral force that is destroyed in everyone going their own way.   Brutality on the afflicted is a process of making psychopaths if it continues unchecked and able to go all the way of completely desensitizing the person. You don't wanna do that. Trust me.   Some of the homeless are interpersonal sociopaths, usually from sexual immorality, stealing, and corrousing, or are initially blank slates. But many of the homeless are the most wonderful people you can ever meet. Real people have been there; in reality and have seen the sickness. They don't want to be a part of that, and that is a blessing from God. The only people I fully trust are homeless.

There is a correlation to my hypothesis about the condition of social neurosis, and how there has been a developmental breakdown in the general population, including the breakdown of the complexity of cognitive structure. There have been a number of streams that show shocking examples of Judges acting childish. One case involves a female judge being dragged out of a courtroom. There is another case in Houston, where a Judge is caught vandalizing his neighbor's car when captured on video. Victim gets probable cause when asking him while recording if he would know why someone would do such a thing.   The judge said it's probably because he keeps parking his car so the bumper sticks out over the sidewalk. Someone who is of adequate social development, would just knock on the neighbors door, and ask him to make sure he's far enough forward when he parks his car. Simple. His actions speak volumes about his state of mind. You might expect to see this sort of behavior with an underdeveloped youth working at the hamburger joint, not a judge for God sake. Wow. Apparently by the judge's own admission, he committed a felony. There is a correlation to some of these authority figures and their behaviors in the history of monarchy such as bully cops. The media is flooded with examples of police forcing people to bow to their authority. What contempt of cop issues really demonstrate, is the same psychological condition of monarchs who were given way too much power. They become addicted to this power, and become enraged when you do not bow to it. They might grant you clemency if you -by your body language and attitude- fully prostrate yourself before their highness. There has been a history of this condition being generated by absolutism. Many of these videos of police escalating situations to provoke reactions correlates to the store employee's hate crime. What they are subconsciously developing, is a familiarity with the limbic system of those who are vulnerable. Safety and security stabilizes our complex limbic system, and keeps us in our right mind. Police officers who have no regard for protocol are terrorist in every form of the definition. Entities endorsing this behavior are expreme terrorists organizations. A police officer can easily -by his extreme amount of unchecked weaponized power- throw someone into survival mode, causing them to experience terror. This drop from L3, destabilizes them emotionally, and causes them to not be able to access their faculties resulting in irrational behavior that they would never do when they are in their right senses in L3. Both the police and store employees are aware of this destabilization, and purposefully trigger them to react to establish grounds for removal. Those who can't hide their homelessness, are often banned from stores by acts of injustice. Security guards are often part of this injustice. They also have 'contempt of cop' issues, when they're not even cops. I've even witnessed them having fun torturing homeless teens and even elderly who have no one to protect their right to live when these vigilante's push them away from the places where they can get food. You don't get many places where you live that take EBT. Be warned everyone; vigilante employees who have no check and balance as to how they are towards the disadvantaged raises levels of desperation that are very dangerous to this society. Exposure pathway becomes a wide gate when gentrification crushes the multitudes as corporatists conquer the land. This exposure will create an army of psychopaths climbing the citadels thirsty for the blood of the elite.   This will be the consequence of the 'nimby' syndrome- the "not in my backyard" group.   This demonstrates that primary self concern puts masses in danger.

Case study- Woodstock 99: So in this small society of Woodstock 99, each strata contributed to the apathy that resulted in anarchy.   Primary role of the police force was to facilitate the exploitation of the spectators, rather than providing safety and protection of the citizens' rights to survive without gouging their vital needs.   Leaders used to have the integrity to take responsibility for the vitality of the society they governed.   If the police facilitate the lock down gouging, then they are responsible for the anarchy that follows.   Public servants' primary role is the safety and wellbeing of the public.   It is in the Constitution that breach of peace by any elected official is punishable by removal of duty.   Promoters and vending companies bear the weight of the responsibility though, that would be using the typical value/means-end rationality that lays out the reason for opportunism to exploit.   Their employees are using substantive rationality that somehow these antisocial norms handed down to them are acceptable..   You have the dynamic of a large number of people, who are in need of sustenance for three days, and are hitt with these insane prices to just gouge the hell out of them, while they are there. But what seems to be the most disturbing level of behavior, was in how the vendors took advantage of people's need to survive to make bank.   That is what was so disturbing about this event.   All interpersonal types seem to be consistent with the liberation pathway.   They are successful, and even charming, but very apathetic on extreme levels. Seems to have no moral charge to their emotion.   On the other hand, the examples of psychopathy are consistent with the exposure pathway, and a few cases show moral charge in their action to emotional dilemmas.   All cases show significant levels of collective fantasy, both primary and secondary types.   As far as Affect- what really stood out about the Woodstock 99 event, was how stark the difference was from Woodstock 69 where volunteers came in with large amounts of water and supplies to help the multitude of kids not of their own.   It proves that the original Woodstock was a phenomenon privy to its time.   One can see the difference in the level of sensitivity within the general population, and the stark contrast to the apathy level of anti socialization, and even the level of collective fantasy.   This example of Woodstock 99's small society was a demonstration and representation of how the sociopaths in the liberation pathway, create the secondary pathway by exposure.   Emotional reaction indicates higher frequencies in moral neural pathways.   Result is violence and destruction.   It literally became a war zone. Decrease in sensitivity of conscience, is in correlation to increase of crime in all forms, even crimes done by lawmakers and law enforcement. But here is an example of a small society where you have a conflict of the two primary pathways; Interpersonal type primarily in the pathway by liberation who are the controlling forces, and the secondary type who are primarily in the pathway by exposure subject to their sociopathic behavior. This account demonstrates the sociopathic lifestyle's effect on the vulnerable who react violently when exposed to their exploits. This correlates with the examples at the camp in Oceanside. You have those at the bottom of the stratus exposed to being traumatized by those who exploit in their liberation without protection and accountability. Gentrification has reached levels of mass destruction. spurious correlation- Loyal fans were being exploited, but attached to their egoes was this collective fantasy. Then suddenly the veil of fantasy is removed, and each one is for himself, KNOWING!, he has no one he can depend on. Independence removes dependability. You're standing out in the baking sun dying of thirst and can't afford water, and they're like "sorry bro". It is this phenomena that reveals the purpose of conscience, which is dependence. The incident at the Woodstock 99 event, is a perfect example of how man depends on others to be sensitive to their conscience, when it comes to their basic needs to survive. Vitality and solidarity are lost without it. Hence, independence is ant-social and the cause of sociopathy.

The crisis only reaches these levels of severity and desperation because of the lack of people depending on each other for survival. You can see how any hope of conscience being able to survive is that they would have to depend on each other. Everyone's for themselves. No one can be depended upon. If dependence is the foundation of our networks, it's not such an emergency, not so much a reason to freak out. No unforeseen oppressive lockdown with merciless gouging of the welfare of the people. This event is an example of a complete 180 degree paradigm shift and the conflict generated by individual independence within this small society of Woodstock 99. Even the structure is instrumental in this exposure. It's no wonder why these trauma survivors out on the streets escape the way they do. The things these people would say to us were horrible. It's quite obvious below the cracks the forces that drive the needle deeper. And it's abused children who get the blame. When you communicate to a youth that they are a criminal because of their homelessness and drug abuse, you communicate to the abused child within, that it was all their fault. The emotional instabilities from brutal beatings, or being molested, or abandoned as a child leaves them in need for others to help. Isolation is the typical pattern that follows. This isolation leaves them out of social progress with their peers, so they do not do well in networking they need to survive when they're grown.

This social disability is the primary reason for lack of employment. Psychotherapists know that the general way you cause someone to relive terror and trauma, is by coming over them. They've been abused and betrayed by those who had authority over them.   The stigma is that they have a problem with authority, when it is because they have been abused by authority. They actually need to be protected from authority, until they get the psychotherapy they need.

Woodstock 99 is also a good example of how attaining money is the primary ethical programming. Even supersedes man's need to survive. Man is only under the illusion of collective fantasy because of his pretension he has from being preoccupied with self indulgence. His selfish ambition plays into the anti-socialization, and the illusion of unity. It's just good business strategy to make people think you're on the same team, while you're exploiting them. Seems to be a method of obscuring the conflict of interest, by stimulating the ego;"bang your head!." This is commodification's impact on the Affect. Some vendors responded to the crowd by reducing prices, but only a small fraction who supply the masses. But still charging money. I'm sure there was some overlooking while people struggled with some level of conscience as these apathetic norms are handed down to them by their bosses. But any musician with a conscience would not have been able to stand that kind of treatment of their fans.   Even loyalty to those who brought the bread and butter, seems non-existent.

I thought the case with Smart-n-Final and Frazier Farms were good examples of anti socialization, how antisocial norms are handed down the stratus to be internalized and enforced. Everyone of them knows in their conscience (if they still have one), that a human being deserves to be treated like one. The apathy increases as we climb the stratus, and so insensitive norms are handed down the stratus for those more sensitive below to adapt to. My friends at both stores have a sense of unity with other employees because they wear the same uniform, but seemed shocked and disturbed about the matter. They could hardly look me in the eye when John wasn't allowed to buy food. Jean Macean was a man arrested in Daytona Beach after brutally stabbing a couple and slashing their throats when they were out riding their bikes in their neighborhood.   People of Daytona Beach were terrified as authorities raced to find him by posting local surveillance footage.   In my observation of what is going on in society right now, he's probably a lone ranger done with injustices like gentrification, where the rich takeover poor neighborhoods, and kick the occupants down the road.   Expect many more like this man. Imagine an army of people like this man, thrown out of their homes and neighborhoods and told to go die somewhere.   1% is building an army against themselves. But it is citizens like this couple, who by their pictures seem to be wonderful people, are going to be the ones paying the consequences for scoundrels conquering the land. Soon none of their cities will be habitable. There's a need for an update on the cause of homelessness since the covid shut-down. There's new quantitative data that has to be researched that are different from that which was reported in the "Shelter from the Storm: Trauma Informed Care in Homeless Service Settings" documentation. I myself have seen on the streets, much more of the 'new homeless' types that are much different than the typical cases.   This term 'new homeless' was used after the housing bubble burst in 2008, and then 2011 when people were even very successful business owners quickly lost their houses, and properties and ended up living in cars and suvs.   I'm seeing much more of these cases, and even where they end up in the drug underworld.   Sassy was the wife of a very successful man who was part of an international trade organization that included political campaigning. Her whole life was being his right hand in all of this. She was even in the presence of other world leaders. She had suddenly ended up with a bone condition that required regular blood transfusions, and then her husband also ended up with a neurological condition that required convalescent care which she was not equipped to handle. The loss of the breadwinner, meant the loss of the entire estate. Her condition led her to pharmaceutical dependency on opiates because of the chronic pain she suffered. Soon after, she had deteriorated in ways that can be expected given the level of loss, without proper emotional and psychological treatment and handling of her situation. Of course, after her new life was settling in that was much different than the one before, she found herself under the cracks with the opiate dependency, and at the mercy of the pharmaceutical companies that just have to make a bajillion dollars off of pills that cost a fraction of a penny.   So now she has to find an affordable alternative that of course is against all the pharmaceutical regulation. So now she has to be a criminal to survive.   She now has to live a life of survival in the harshest of environments in constant terror.   After getting to know her on a personal level, she even was forthcoming about her own guilt of lying and playing men in a certain way to survive without "putting out." I could see how the levels of her desensitization had to do with her having to live under this level of exposure.   A woman suddenly on the streets is so vulnerable I just can't hardly explain it. The level of terror they experience, and the level of exploitation of their vulnerability is astronomical. There is no way of explaining it. After all of this, someone who doesn't even know you or your life is screaming at you and calling you a whore.   Sassy has been deemed by the entire system as 'life not worthy of life.'   She could have probably been able to recover if her problems weren't just left for her to deal with. No net to catch you. Corporatist fascists refuse to allow anything social that would be able to catch us in these ways because they demand unfettered acquisition on all properties. They can't have that ability, if the system is set up socially. They demand and require antisocialism.

Postal worker Jennifer San Marco from Galetta California. From my experience with trauma, I could tell right away when I heard it. I immediately was correlating it to Son of Sam in 1976 because both experienced a disruption in attachment during vital developmental years. Disruption in attachment is one of the most devastating emotional wounds and usually resulting in psychological fragmentations and sufferings that are severe. I was then shocked to see after already forming this probability in her case, that she had developed an interest in the Son of Sam story that appeared in some of her writings. This told me she had made a personal connection with him that she never had on a very deep level of pain. What compounded her disruption in attachment when her parents divorced, was that her very close friend was lost in this disruption. She then followed -what could be expected in these extreme cases- a pattern in which she creates an imaginary friend who replaces the lost one. This correlates to my hypothesis about the escape by imaginary form of trauma induced psychosis. This is an expected result given the isolation that occurs on this level of trauma. This then stunts their cognitive structure, and then without meeting the emergency of her being able to process this devastation, she had no one to help her find the 'why' in it all. That is when reprocessing happens, when in the recall they process a healthy 'why' that can put their soul at peace. Without this vital need of having someone there in it with her, she was left to whatever 'why' that her experiences and imagination would ascribe. These influences have the potential to send someone like her into a state of unbearable torment in her soul. She in many ways was quietly screaming for help in her behavior, that was misinterpreted and labeled as just mental illness. Somehow, she found someone who knew her torment that she could relate to. Spree killings are from what I can tell, a commitment they have made as they've come to the conclusion they can no longer live in this evil world. It is an addendum to a suicide pact with oneself, and sometimes others, to rid what is in their mind the cause of their hell. This is the danger of them not having someone there in their life, to be in it with them on a secret level to help them find the right 'why', that would put their soul at peace and heal their devastating wounds. Intimacy is by definition, a relationship in which we share our hidden secrets. Jennifer was in dire need of this, but denied it by the society she was born into where everyone is left to their own pain and problems. So the attack is more on the society, and particular roles that key characters play in this nightmare they've found themselves in with no way of escape. C.P.S., (child protective services), has been causing devastating trauma to children by suddenly grabbing them and

129

tearing them from the arms of their loved ones as they scream in horror. They do this without due justification, and somehow these social workers were given the power of judges to inflict the same wounds that brought about serial killers. For what they do to children and their parents, we can all be expecting an army of Sons of Sams and Jennifers and Jean Maceans making their suicide pacts. It doesn't matter what is in their urine, you don't ever disrupt a vital attachment of a child to their parents. Ever! Get ready. Now it's pay day- that toll we didn't see coming for slime balls ruling the land. Simple stuff. Don't have to be no brain surgeon. When it comes to the liberation pathway of sociopaths, and the exposure pathway of violent psychopaths, it's just simple math. 1 plus 1 is 2. Exposing people to the terror of slime balls ruling the land, equals crazy enraged killers wanting to end it all, and burn it all down, and kill everyone. Is there supposed to be some other expectation? Another case of how the rational mind has problems with simple elementary math.

When the cost of fuel went to an all time high as policies seem to exploit the vulnerable, Stephen Colbert said "a clean conscience is worth a buck or two." Then they all started cheering and laughing. "Yayyyyy" (American hero). The atmosphere after his marvelous one-liner suddenly became really light about the devastating situation. And it showed how his idea of "conscience" somehow wasn't including empathy for those struggling to stay barely above the cracks. "What about the 99?" "Who cares?" Mr. Colbert, the conscience is the awareness of that part in us that cares about people. If genuine concern and care isn't there, then It's just an ethical programming that's replacing the actual "conscience." Under this guise of 'conscience', the 99% could totally end up falling into utter destitution and ruin from this unbelievable level of greed, but the 1% can still have a clean conscience? What the fff*^#doh?????? This spike in fuel cost probably will add to the number of those displaced by an action that would 'retain your clean conscience'??! OMG. Can you even have a conscience and say that? I don't know. Is independence affordable?- social dependence is for those who can't afford, or function in the competitiveness of individual independence. But capitalism refuses them to have a system where they can enjoy normal social existence feeling safe and secure, that their hard work all their life isn't going to land them in poverty and marked as 'life not worthy of life.' That is what I'm documenting; people can work hard their whole life, even serve in war, and just end up deemed 'life not worthy of life.' How in the hell is that not betrayal?? Each, no matter how damaged, is forced to depend on only themselves until they become destitute. I've seen a totally blind man, left to survive in a dog-eat-dog society. These societies become hell when the structure burns the edict of peace. And that is what has happened. Again; the contract in this society that replaced the patriarchy of depending on our clans, has been totally incinerated. Now there is no remedy. No recourse. No way to undo what has been done. The looter has taken loot, and the trader has betrayed. Now there's nothing but hell for them to pay.

Cognitive breakdown is a social breakdown- rational fantasy brings strong illusions of people cheating on us when they're not. Or vise-versa; illusions of someone not cheating on you when they are. This tumultuous force in relationships, is from them not getting the confirmation from a close relation of common interests that all are accountable too. So the eyes are on the 'us', versus the individual. It is these UNaccountable spheres around our personal lives that makes people generally feel unsafe for family preservation, and even get to the point of hyper protectiveness, that is demonized in the confusion of what is going on. I've seen a lot of people screaming at someone for betraying them, when they were doing the same thing. But when you are helping people with pain and are separate from their biases, you find some cases where both are condemning the other for something neither one of them were doing. "You've been cheating on me you *&*#^." I've known some of these cases, and it was sad to see someone hurt in this way after they were so faithful. We are idiots when we rely on our own perspective and understanding that independence has us so confident in. Sociological perspective has to create the right imagination by vantage points trusted in. Usually involving other perspectives accountable to each other. This is also a cognitive structure breakdown, by lack of healthy networking. People are freaking out and screaming about things generated by the impairment of this breakdown. Pharmacy is making a killing off of this social neurosis from a system that forces us to just go get some more drugs, to go in conjunction with all the lobbying to keep us in our own little cells which denies our networking of dependence. Social networks are supposed to bring support you can depend on. Now it's just, we support in a way that does not support people. If a crisis comes, they watch you fall through the cracks while blowing cash. They only support the party bill, not the survival bill. Networking isn't 'I'm going to a box where others meet to play with our toys.' Or, 'I'm going to watch one dimensional images of faces that giggle at each other.' Corporatism wants you to believe that's all you need. They've dwindled down the meaning of social networking, to be some sort of anti-socialization in a sandbox with toddlers playing with their toys who all depend on the big 'daddy.' Things have only gotten so bad, because everyone has just been trying to negotiate with sociopaths who believe everything is for them, while still going along because of their own selfishness.   It's like trying to negotiate policy reform with the best of the dog-eat-dogs. Their ways of dealing with problems via voter registration, ruin our ability to solve any of the problems that this mad frenzy of consumption hunger has created. You will only give them more leverage against anything you are trying to do to solve our crisis that is sinking our ship. It's like a way of them forcing you to give up all your plans and strategies, for them to act preemptively behind the scenes against what you're trying to do. They see that fighting for our rights is actually criminal. And so of course, they always got the real deal going on behind the curtain so we don't ruin everything because of our incompetence. They see that their excessive acquisition is evidence of their greatness and superiority in decision making when it's just because they are the most conniving and the best at it. Their ethic is in their competition to have the most, and that we need to just be good 'losers,' and not complain about them taking all the land, rights, and resources on the planet for their small little click to squander. They see it was a fair game, and that they're the fair winners.

Forcing the poor into isolation, and denying them support networks- A couple who was at my camp, ended up on the voucher list, and got a motel room right next door to my room. After forcing her into isolation, where she wasn't allowed to have her man who supports her, and protects her, or even her dog with her. After it not working out because they were tearing her away from her daughter to put her in some suicide chamber. She just ended up back in Oceanside and with her supporter and protector; the man she chooses to be with in her life. McAlister had to tell them both the bad news; there is nothing for couples in the housing, or sheltering programs.   CPS took her daughter from her, which devastated them both because she was homeless. After doing everything they said to do, and having all these social services and court proceedings, she still wasn't able to get her back because of her housing situation. All the money that was spent on this process of disrupting an attachment between a mother, and her daughter, could have gone to just housing them. This is all because of the criminalization of people who don't have enough money to survive in this high cost of living. Now they both are emotionally wrecked in the exact ways that scientific research has determined to be as to the cause of chronic homelessness and drug abuse. That means, the system is creating chronic homelessness and drug abuse because of the ways that they barge our private lives and tear our families apart. There's something about tearing poor families apart and sending them to Mexico where they're leaking Fentanyl that seems Draconic. Draconic is a legislative act created by 1%, to legalize killing all those not useful for their agendas. Gentrification has a suicide plan for all you ready to fall through the cracks.

Conclusion- If conscience is the means to the ends of dependence, then independence is a replacement of the ends, that now requires a new means. Means are replaced by new means to meet the new ends, which is independence. So the conscience is for dependence- each having that sensitivity to others living in them, an internal governance having a strong influence in decisions being made so it can all work. Sociopathy is the means for independence; I don't have to worry about anyone else but me, and I don't have to feel bad that I'm wasting money while others suffer, even family members. I can do anything I want without someone giving me a guilt trip about it. The liberal club is- 'only those who don't bring drama about all the slime.' Commodification has gone to a slimy level while trying to make selfishness work out well. But of course we know it doesn't really work out in independence, so we have to lie, cheat, play the game no matter the cost to others, cuz it can't really work in the "real world" if we're totally open and honest. These are some of the more common rationalizations in society. The collective conscience sees, and it goes with collective tradition, that a boy getting a little too big to still be in the "mine" stage of development, poses a threat to the entire clan. He must find contentment with his portion, his fair share. The threat can be seen in his interactions with other children; the violence generated by his continual violation of grabbing and saying "mine", while other children react with hitting and scratching, and pulling to get it back. Crossing the will of the child by necessary means of discipline is criminalized. Law seems to enforce the immediate response to the child's selfish demands for gratification. These anti spanking laws just happened to feed the market's demand of mass consumption, and bring many customers to the prison industrial complex, because undisciplined children are deviant and rebellious to laws and constraints to stimulating their senses as they please. The more I tried to get programs and nonprofits to work with me, the more I could see that it's all just about people having their personal 501C3's rather than finding solutions. Solutions were just not going with the regular routine, and so were just discarded to allow the problem to continue. The more people tried to make a big deal about me, the more it was messing up my peer support for those I'm trying to help. I found more and more, people around these needy hurt ones, who have the attitude that they are above homelessness. The last person you want on the homeless service team are people that see that they are above being homeless. This is an indication that they are not bringing the empathy needed to 'sterilize' the setting for protecting the afflicted. It is proven that they need a peer approach. A peer is someone on your level, not above you. It is impossible to have white coats and badges as part of trauma informed care.   This is to protect the industry that police have been feeding. They terrorize those traumatized until they're acting like psychos, and then they feed them into the mental health pharmaceutical monster to devour them.   This rakes in piles of cash going to the problem. So they all work in conjunction including the churches that have this 'above homelessness' Jesus. Demonization co opting with criminalization. The ones needing to have the say so for this approach, are demerited by the system that stifles their ability to bring the necessary solutions as 'not qualified.' Christopher Rodriguez determined my approach to be "irresponsible" during city council.   The apathetic continue to rule while subjecting these victims to even more devastating levels of exposure, and see that there is nothing to be fixed although the problem becomes a catastrophe.   It is because it is forced to be in the hands of those who bring gentrification. Gentrification: *"the process whereby the character of a poor urban area is changed by wealthier people moving in, improving housing, and attracting new businesses. Typically displacing current inhabitants in the process." (web dictionary.)*   This problem has creeped in as the percentage of ownership has dwindled down to a small few. Now it's a real problem since 1% has been owning everything; gentrification has been able to conquer the land and even push families out of the neighborhoods they grew up in for generations. That manipulation from the outside has been happening in Oceanside California. Big money was able to just walk in and nullify the whole city council. It was abundantly clear- not even citizens or even the mayor had much to say so about anything. It was when the grand hotels moved in, and raised the cost of our living. Much of us were pushed through cracks, and they kicked us down the road while new money moved in. The owner of a breakfast restaurant that had been there for years, that hung some of my stained-glass art in his window was brutally told he's just gotta 'shut down and move out.' Having to shut down and move out of town was survival.   The hard work of a man with a family had no constitutional right. All the family effort, and security was compromised by corporate giants. Proven fact. Not an opinion.   Many of those compromised in this displacement will find no refuge in other cities if they fall through cracks in the process.   At this point, they find out they don't really have any land to belong to.   No right to even live anywhere.   The cities taking them in, really see that the problem of these displaced people are not the cities problem.   At this revelation of losing the right to live, you generally freak out and start having emotional outbursts in public.   Now you've entered the 'mentally ill' class that no one should really pay any attention to. You go to a church for food, and they tell you that you're in this situation because you aint got it right with

Jesus. So if you just get it right with Jesus, he's gonna bless you too. After hearing your pain and suffering, they tell you we can't make excuses for what's happened to us, and start to throw all these principals at you because you obviously lack moral fiber, and then tell you while you're squatting in a bush, "get a job." This is where the new homeless discover that you need a place to live to have a job. But none of the idiots yelling at you to get a job have this simple understanding. Their rational development in a pecking order type of society has dwindled their minds down to that of chickens, who are quicker to peck the seed than the runt who doesn't get enough. The bigger chickens start to get annoyed with the runt at the bottom of the pecking order, and start pecking at them to torture them so they will leave. But the runt is trying to survive. I've experienced this phenomenon while working with chickens on farms. Runts were even pecked to death by those having more than they needed. In my own experience, I've seen a common occurrence with people who were homeless. There is a hate crime, where employees who hate them know how to trigger them by acts of cruelty, and then justify banning them from the store where they need to get vitals. This breakdown of vitality is the biggest threat to all cities burning down to the ground overnight. It will happen. A city without mercy, will surely burn. I've experienced even recently- a deli in a store serving me a sandwich that had ten times too much mayo that created a disgusting mess I could hardly eat. In the same store, I walk up to look at the price of some meat and a punk employee just moves in and stops me, even sticking his arm in my face to reach some meat on the other side of where I was standing. It was such a blatant and aggressive act, my old violent trigger would have greatly hurt that young man. But I was thankful God gave me power to not react. Thank you God. I want to wait for his mighty hand to deal with the situation. Everyone just above the cracks, be warned. These corporations don't care that they were made wealthy by your hard earned money, or if you even served in war for their freedom to acquire. There are many wonderful homeless people pecked at, and tortured to get them to go away from the watering hole they need to survive. The freedom they've been spreading around, has 1% taking everything for themselves as masses are pushed through cracks only to fall into the category of 'life not worthy of life.' We all need to face the reality,-allowing slimeballs to run the show has become a norm, and there are consequences for allowing sociopath's to have free reign to acquire all the exchange medium while leaving victims of child abuse, war, and opportunism on the vulnerable, out in the cold. What the slimeballs depend on to keep their iron fist on the helm, is our own individual independence. That is the facilitation that removes all subjection to accountability. What it comes down to is; they fight to avoid the socialism that would rescue the needy, so they can keep their free market going to become even more lavished with wealth, and more elaborate tech toys. They're trying to keep the party going, when it should have ended a long time ago. There's a toll bridge for playing when we should be preparing for the famine. This tyranny was warned to come, and now it is here in stark reality. Face it with the fear of God, because his anger is coming for this tyranny, and all the injustice. Look. It is already coming upon them now. Anyone in it with them, is going down in the same flames they are. Have nothing to do with them. We must be set free within, because it is a violent and horrendous day coming to bring down these cruel tyrants. They can't stand against the universe who is here to claim the whole planet. The messiah is at the gate, and preparing to enter. We few who care, must all surrender to God and let his mighty hand do the smiting. And fear that mighty one who can flick all these giants to the other side of the universe. What they have is toys compared to what is before them at this very moment. Deep down, they probably already know it. There is a way the meek inherit the earth. The situation with the sociology professor is more of what is going on above the professor. It is a representation of what is going on with the University, more than just the instructor. It was like charging people a lot of money, for something that wasn't genuinely provided. That's how it is, I'm seeing people with badges and titles on doors and name tags, but generally incompetent to do any of the jobs. This goes all the way from shopping clerk, to the leaders of the nation. It is all the result of the rational mind removing critical standards from society. To a social psychologist, this is a clear indication of a breakdown in cognitive structuring which includes the vital functions of critical problem solving. Here the sociology professor and students in my class were trying to find solutions to the conflicts in society, without using any critical thought of the pillars of sociology to find solutions. The removal of this subjectivity even cuts off students who have sufficient cognitive complexity, from having access to these critical perspectives that we need for problem solving. When critical standards are removed, we lose our ability to solve problems, period. The genuine standard of services and production plummets as Affect is being desensitized in general population. It is by the moral force of the collective conscience, that would determine the quality of the product you are selling. America had once prided itself on its quality of engineering at a reasonable price. Cars were built to last over a century. Now they cost enormous amounts of money for junk that will hardly last a decade. Parts aren't even rebuildable, everything is disposable. This is the problem with having no moral force in the governance of society.. This is how the anti socialization has gone to the point where the big money has you depending on things to live, that are destroying the entire planet. So of course to adapt- you have to be desensitized to the point of not even caring about destroying the entire planet. Planetary genocide becomes part of homeostasis. Whatever caring you have, is being desensitized by the continual destruction and murder on a global level. But in our fantasy, it's all the bankers and politicians fault. In reality, we are all the cogs in this social annihilator- this apparatus of mass destruction. We have a choice. We have to suffer to make it right. We all have to repent, take up our cross, and bear it with Yahshua in serving, rather than being served- starting with the runt on the street. Heaven is a place where everyone loves each other, and serves each other daily leaving no one out. Heaven on earth isn't parasitic cities that produce nothing, and consume all the resources. That is hell on earth. What do we want? This perspective brings me to the conclusion that cultivating and guarding this vital need of conscience is primary to the safety and prosperity of society, and ultimately the survival of the planet. Even bringing about environments that have meaningful relationships that are genuine, and transparent which come about in common areas instead of solitary confinement. Affection is only established by togetherness in life's struggles in the provision of needs, and pleasant moments of being in harmony because you are together in this journey. This is lost by people becoming commodities to each other, each using the other for self interests. Should we not be ashamed of ourselves? This growing dis-concern has affected the ecosystem even to threaten global catastrophe, which demonstrates the serious level of the condition on a macro level. *"His health is demonstrated in his harmony with the ecosystem from which he emerged (Sane Society)"* The common conscience seems to have been a nuisance to the goal of attaining all that can be had in a capitalistic society, and had to be removed in order to adapt. Affection is out of order in the common workplace, school, society in general. If you can find a time and place, you'll have to schedule it which is kind of inAffective. When the necessity of dependence leaves us with the option of practicality or love, we're generally left feeling unneeded and unloved, with our own stuff. Great! It all goes to show that Aristotle's rationalization that private property gives us the opportunity to share, doesn't mean anything when no one wants to share anymore. If they do share, somehow it always ends up that the needy aren't in on this sharing. Which brings into question the motive for their "sharing". The only way is if self pursuit is abandoned for the sake of humanity.

Humanist's proposal- REPENT!! We must all repent of our selfishness, and realize the hell it's created. Return to what God intended; a boy learning to gather for others, rather than himself. Return to what brings life on earth, and remove what doesn't, *"must so organize industry that the instrumental character of economic activity is emphasized by its subordination to the social purpose for which it is carried on."* [sane society pg 219] We first need to come out of the grand illusion, and into the reality of the devastation that we have neglected the social needs of our children for the sake of progress. Unless we do this, we remain in the fantasy of precontemplation as we rationalize away our reality and the condition worsens.   Durkheim established that the moral force originated from collective living. But where or when are we supposed to do this in our society? Corporatism even prohibits us from loving people when they need it. These traits have been dying since the beginning of our golden age. If we create a "dog eat dog" society, we should expect it to end with everyone eating each other. What are we expected to get out of it, a nation of people who all get along even though they use each other like commodities? If you don't care about me, and my problem is not in your backyard, why should I care about you? Who are you going to turn to after all this nimby-onic attitude when catastrophe comes? We have yet to determine if this structured society even allows for Affect. Rationality's impact on Affect leaves us with the obvious conclusion; it has the potential to go to the furthest extent of complete Affectual flatline. Antithesis to Karssanti's conclusion.

Antibodies- "Antibodies are specialized, Y-shaped proteins that bind like a lock-and-key to the body's foreign invaders — whether they are viruses, bacteria, fungi or *parasites. They are the "search" battalion of the immune system's search-and-destroy system, tasked with finding an enemy and marking it for destruction."* There are antibodies for these pathogens of the rational mind. There is a restorer of spirit, and who has the authority to drive out evil invaders who possess us to do things not in our heart. Because the influence of biblical scriptures didn't involve the institutions of church, I wasn't indoctrinated with their theoretical perspectives. I simply read scripture, and looked up the definitions of the words. A psychologist once told me it was this influence that led me to fixating my mind on wholesome thoughts. He contributed this to keeping me from following the typical path that the general people who suffer my level of trauma would take- which is generally we end up dead from such a violent life, or lifers in prison. God's word was my recovery from psychopathy, and will always be. It all comes down to Yahshua being the doctor, because the Prophets and Apostles wrote what God's living spirit was telling them to write.

His word is living (Heb 4:12). He is his living word that you can write down and send to someone. We either seek his mind about things, or don't. According to our initial created purpose, we are out of our mind if we aren't in his. But my confession is; the word of God was able to restore a very damaged and tormented soul, and give him a heart to care.   That is the whole point– if we care. The greatest miracle God could do, is to restore a soul so that they could love people; especially the needy. Isn't that what the world has been crying out for; leaders who would actually love even the poor and lead with righteousness? The curse is that the prince of this world refuses to allow the money to be put into the hands of those who are just and true, and who genuinely care. It seems anyone trying to lead with justice and impartiality with genuine care, are set up for a big rejection. They are a part of the foundational stones of the first corner stone- the stone the builders rejected. He said, 'if they rejected me, they will reject you.' His servants are the faithful ones who do not put their own needs before the needs of the clan. They seek justice for the smallest ones. This has always been a conflict with the established authority of those who have all the money. And so it has always been the need for someone to deny themselves and confront authority, and risk their own banishment. That is the same in collectives, the poorer ones are the most likely to be the most humble sensitive ones. That is why the discipleship was an opposition to mammon ruling the clan. It had to be, that God's word would supersede, and they would all bow to his word. God's wrath came on the premise that the people just bowed to the money, and didn't care what God was wanting them to do. Those wondering why I did all this, need to understand that it was coming from a deep conviction that brought me to a place of repentance with deep sorrow because of the horrible fruit of my own life. And then in trying to give it up, I ended up part of the worst denomination in the history of Christianity. To do God's will commanded by Yahshua, that life had to die. It had to be destroyed so that something from him could come about. I know his mind and heart is the only thing that is going to bring about good fruit. All the scriptures in the New Testament are his blue-prints for a life of love and happiness. It's not so hard to interpret, when we stop trying to apply it to self life. Once that is gone, then all the scriptures are revealed. So it started with John the Baptist, setting the way straight. What has been omitted in large part of the message, was the foundation of it. Yahshua was baptized into John's ministry of repentance. That is why John was confused about baptizing him. But Yahshua said, let all righteousness be accomplished. John's baptism of water was a baptism of repentance. And when the people said "what shall we do," John brought the attention to the orphan who didn't even have a tunic. Saying "let the one who has two tunics, share with the one who has none, Luke 3:8" This was the repentance of self life, that left the needy with not even enough to survive. This correlates to the apostles being instructed by Yahshua about having one tunic and one cloak while they were being disciplined in the way. This is so they could receive treasure in heaven no one could steal, that would make them content to be able to be entrusted with the welfare of the needy without it being plundered by thieves. This was all a part of what he commanded them in Luke 12:33, to go and sell all their possessions, and create a purse that will never wear out. This would be known as the 'common purse,' that was for the poor (Anointing at Bethany John 12). So he commanded his disciples to do what he did, and what he told the rich young ruler he must do to enter heaven. *"It is easier for a camel to enter the eye of a needle, than for a rich man to enter the kingdom."* When the apostles asked *"who can be saved?"* Then Yahshua said *"with man it is impossible, but with God all things are possible."* This was proven on the day of Pentecost, when 3,000 gave up their lives, "from time to time, those who owned lands and properties sold them and brought all the money from the sales and laid it all down at the feet of the apostles (Acts 4:32-)." The words "from time to time," means that in all the times of people coming and laying it all down, some were rich and had land and properties. It usually was those who didn't have much to give. It was easy for them. So this was to show that even the rich were able to be saved, which was impossible on their own efforts. That's why it takes all our efforts at the same time. The Holy Spirit was initially sent to those who left their own life, and were together in one accord. Not in their own lives. But it is in this act of laying it all down in your heart first, that brings about the power of his blood to do what I can't do in my own power. That is the power of his blood that removes all sin. We spill our own in it, if we share in his sacrifice. His word is living and active in taking up the cross of his sacrifice and bearing it. Yahshua is very compassionate, and merciful. His salvation in our lives, begins by the cleansing of the conscience by confessing and repenting. This is what the thief on the cross did just before he died. He accepted his guilt, and thought his punishment to be just as he acknowledged Yahshua's innocence. Not even thinking to include himself in the paradise that Yahshua was heading for, he hoped to just be remembered. But Yahshua saw that his heart was saved just in time, and had a reward even though he didn't have the chance to change his life. Salvation is a simple matter of the heart, not a scientific achievement. It all comes by faith that grows as you hear his word daily, and believe in the ones he sent to you, to know his heart. James 4:1 "What causes fights and quarrels among you? Are they not from the desires that war within you?" What starts a war?

Job 8:14-15 correlates to the treachery of organic solidarity vs mechanical where dependence on each other creates a solid foundation in which to build. That is our initial motivation to work, that creates a network one can rely on; one that will hold them in times of trouble.

Analogy explaining the treachery of organic solidarity:

"*What they trust in is fragile*

   what they rely on is a spider's web

They lean on it but it gives way

   they cling to it but it does not hold them

Symbolic interaction- the growth in varieties of symbols in flags, logos, emblems, etc are examples of an established contrarianism, it's only us and you're not a part of us, so you are not our concern. This is an example of the indifference that results from the individuation. This is the Achilles heel that collapses this organic solidarity. Coexistence depends on adequate similarities and common grounds to develop thresholds of tolerance for each other. Individuation poses a threat to this coexistence. As individuation broadens spectrums, we lose this relatedness and common ground.

Dramaturgical- Parable of the Patriarch: There once was a patriarch of a large clan, who left the eldest in charge of the whole estate while he was gone. The patriarch was gone so long, the clan thought he wasn't to return, though a few kept praying and hoping. After many years, he suddenly arrived un-announced, but was shocked and heartbroken to find there were some of the family members living in squalor outside the camp; dirty, hungry, and cold. Even some of the elders were among them. When the patriarch went into the camp, he found the strongest of them eating the choicest portions, and indulging on the resources, while some were serving them as slaves. The patriarch was infuriated at this, and with his staff, he severely beat those who were being served, stripped them of their garments, and banished them from the land. The patriarch went to those who were left in squalor, and forced to serve, and he comforted them with his love. And they had the most glorious feast there ever was.

v. Interpretative Framework

Social structure of chickens. Rules of the roost- too many roosters create havoc and fighting; males fighting over the females, and hens suffering from the roosters pecking at them to control them. Individuals create a chicken coop as they focus on themselves and their own needs. This creates a pecking order in which our souls are corrupted and social existence is replaced by helter skelter. Psychologically we slowly develop the mind of animals; creatures of instinct without love. Everyone striving for their personal status in the pecking order creates a hostile and dangerous environment.

Schindler's List: I could have saved one more (ending scene) Full HD - YouTube Example of awakening, and restoration of the soul that brings awareness of the spirit.

//www.youtube.com/watch?v=NS4UT_t73b0

Lord of the Flies- rational construct leads to social destruct.

Grinch Stole Christmas (exposure wound of being excluded for differences. Example of corrective emotional responses after acceptance and forgiveness. Articulates on processing)

It's A Wonderful Life and A Christmas Carol (examples of an awakening from fantasy and the traumatic impact. And the shift in attitude of affect and change in behavior)

1975 movie Stepford Wives- A pharmaceutical millionaire orchestrates an illusion of utopia. Liberal wives are secretly being made into automatons. Correlates to hypothesis in the analogy of the motive for doppelganger by adaptation to remove critical standard.

McGOUGH

www.ingramcontent.com/pod-product-compliance
Lightning Source LLC
Chambersburg PA
CBHW061149030426

42335CB00003B/154